How to Open a Financially Successful

Specialty Retail & Gourmet Foods Shop

With Companion CD-ROM

Sharon Fullen and Douglas R. Brown

How to Open a Financially Successful Specialty Retail & Gourmet Foods Shop

Atlantic Publishing Group, Inc.
1210 SW 23rd Place
Ocala, Florida 34474
800-541-1336
352-622-5836 - Fax

www.atlantic-pub.com - Web site
sales@atlantic-pub.com - E-mail

SAN Number :268-1250

International Standard Book Number: 0-910627-32-0

Library of Congress Cataloging-in-Publication Data

Brown, Douglas Robert, 1960-
How to open a financially successful specialty retail & gourmet foods shop : with companion CD-ROM / by Douglas Robert Brown.
p. cm.
ISBN 0-910627-32-0 (alk. paper)
1. New business enterprises. 2. New business enterprises--Management.
3. Food industry and trade. 4. Specialty stores. I. Title.

HD62.5.B7623 2004
381'.456413'00681--dc22

2004008414

Printed in the United States

Book cover, layout and design by Meg Buchner of Megadesign
www.mega-designs.com • e-mail: megadesn@mchsi.com

Table of Contents

Chapter 1 Starting Your Own Gourmet Store

Chapter 2 Launching Your Business

Chapter 3 The Basics of Buying a Gourmet Shop

Chapter 4 How to Invest in a Franchise

Chapter 5 Planning for Success—Writing a Business Plan

Chapter 6 Launching Your Business—Pre-Opening Activities

Chapter 7 Successful Employee Relations and Labor Cost Control

Chapter 8 Your Customers

Chapter 9 Marketing Your Business

Chapter 10 Public Relations: How to Get Customers in the Door

Chapter 11 Choosing Your Sales Mix

Chapter 12 Equipping Your Store

Chapter 13 Public Areas of Your Store

Chapter 14 Back-of-the-Store Work Areas

Chapter 15 Creating a Safe and Productive Environment

Chapter 16 Your Store Staff

Chapter 17 Purchasing

Chapter 18 Cash Flow

Chapter 19 Financial Management and Budgeting

Chapter 20 Basic Cost Control for Retail Operations

Chapter 21 Controlling Your Labor Costs

Chapter 22 Leaving Your Retail Business

Chapter 23 Resources

Starting Your Own Gourmet Store

The specialty (or gourmet) food industry continues to grow at a steady pace regardless of the state of the economy. In fact, budget-trimming for some folks means dining out less and creating gourmet meals at home instead. This shift of dollars means business opportunities for you!

Operating an independent retail store is hard work. Your success depends upon your entrepreneurial skills along with excellent research. Realizing your dream can be an exceptionally rewarding endeavor—personally and professionally. The ingredients for success go well beyond an elegantly appointed store or the best names in cutlery; they are a complex blend of passion, vision, risk-taking and business acumen.

Solidifying Your Vision

Your dream of owning your own business sparks your quest, but creating a solid vision of how you want to accomplish your dream is the foundation of success. Creating a vision will help you write your business plan, sell your concept to lenders and potential investors, and communicate your desires and needs to architects, contractors, designers and suppliers.

To follow are some ways to help you solidify your vision. This understanding will help you make decisions when faced with compromises, budgetary problems and unforeseen obstacles.

Ways to Explore Your Passion

Close your eyes. Can you see your dream operation? Are the glass displays filled with artfully arranged cooking utensils? Do regulars come in just to see what is new? Do people enjoy tasting your samples? These images all represent your passion.

- Take a few hours of uninterrupted time to think over your personal and financial reasons for committing your energies and "nest egg," taking on a partner or tying yourself to a long-term loan. It takes time to become profitable—are you prepared financially and emotionally for this investment?
- Create a list of the positives and negatives of being in business for yourself. Every venture has risk (negatives), but the positives should outweigh them. If your entrepreneurial spirit is not dampened by the potential risks, your next step is to give your vision a voice.
- Determine what talents you can bring to the process. Do you love searching for exciting new food products, or are you more interested in selling? Do you want to let hired design professionals handle the details, or do you prefer to be consulted on every detail from the front door to the receiving door?

What Do You Want Your Store to Be?

Since you are reading this book, we can assume that you are a "foodie"—someone who reads cookbooks, enjoys trying new restaurants, has all the latest cooking gadgets or travels 85 miles round trip for the perfect loaf of

French bread. In other words—you have the passion!

Now turn your thoughts to selling "your passion." What do you want to sell and how will you go about it? Retail stores come in many different sizes, shapes and styles, and there are thousands of choices on what you could stock and how you could present it.

Before you can start developing your business and marketing plans (see Chapter 5), you need to sit down and write a thorough description of what your store will look like, what kinds of products you will carry and who will want to buy these products. Every decision from this day forward will be based upon that definition. However, because this definition is based upon assumptions and unknowns, you will be redefining and fine-tuning it along the way. If you do not revise this definition, it probably means that you have not thoroughly researched your business prospects and customer needs.

Remember, this is a definition from the heart—not based on research at this point. When you close your eyes, can you mentally walk up and down the aisle and see what your customers will see?

- **Write a one-minute "elevator pitch."** If you found yourself in an elevator with a wealthy investor, how would you describe your vision (and secure the cash) in the time it takes to travel up 20 floors? Show your passion while emphasizing the tangible benefits.

Your Store Could Be...

Imagine what your store will look like—this is called merchandising. How you merchandise your products directly affects the crowd you attract, creates perceived values of your wares and increases your sales per customer visit.

Your store should reflect your personality and your interests. If you love home-style foods and sunflowers, your store could have a casual, comfortable feeling. If you are a "dress for dinner" person, perhaps the classic black and white (with a dash of red) is more like a store you would want to share with others.

When you research your ideal customer and demographics, you will need to be certain that your merchandising style suits their expectations. If your style does not connect with your potential customer base, they will not be coming in or returning to your store. You may find that your store's appearance needs to change somewhat. However, beware that creating a store that feels "alien" to you may be a warning sign.

Your product offerings may "demand" a specific look. For example, a store featuring "hot stuff" begs for a stimulating red décor. (We will discuss merchandising and "theme" décor in Chapter 13.)

Products

Your store's products can range from carrying a broad selection of gourmet food to featuring a single food type, such as jams, to emphasizing one genre of food, such as Cajun, or selling only small kitchen gadgets. What you sell is your store's lifeblood.

Every industry has a sales cycle. For example, you will probably complete your winter season product ordering in late summer. By understanding this cycle, you will be able to have stock arrive when you need it and take advantage of manufacturers' early buy programs.

Gourmet retail stores are a great blend of the practical, the trendy and the "must have." Food is a necessity for life, yet no one really "needs" 40 different kinds of imported olive oil. Food trends may hit the coasts and never reach middle America, or they can be a fantastic new twist to a favorite food. Gourmet "must haves" are a merchandiser's dream—simply point them out and they will fly off the shelves.

Niche Markets

Selling gourmet food and food-related products is a "niche" market, since an equivalent is probably readily available at every grocery store in your community. However, the interest in all things food continues to grow. (We will talk about niches within the gourmet category later in the book.)

As opposed to offering a huge range for food and food-related products, your store could focus on a niche market—a segment of interest to fewer people, yet with enough interest to have sufficient sales. This niche could be a wine shop, a store featuring only locally produced food items or only Oriental food products.

It is especially important when serving a niche market that you are an expert in your offering. If you are not the expert, you must have one who is a part of your management team. Your entire staff will need to be well trained and capable of working with "demanding" customers and "newbies." The majority of customers you are attracting will be well informed and have an expectation of your knowledge and expertise. In addition, to broaden your customer base, you want to bring in people who will rely on your expert advice to guide them with their purchasing decisions.

Limiting Your Offerings

As you stock your store for the first time, you will soon realize you have to make choices and set limits. Simply walking the aisle of the annual International Home and Housewares Show in Chicago will overwhelm you with possibilities. Spend a day at a regional Gourmet Food and Gift Show or Confectioner's Association show and you will go away stuffed and eager to buy everything! So how do you choose? By researching your competition! See what they carry and what they are missing. The better you understand your market and customer base, the more capable you will be in selecting the right items for your store.

Remember that you will be tying up the majority of your working capital on stocking inventory so it is important that you make wise decisions. Every retailer in America makes purchasing errors (remember, that's how all those outlet malls started). They misinterpret the demand, receive merchandise after the trend passes or they don't understand how to properly market the product. The key is minimizing these mistakes as much as possible. (Later in this book, we'll discuss how to keep "in touch" with customer needs.)

Not only will you have to decide what to buy, you have to determine how much to stock of a specific item. You'll need to factor in order/delivery times and the "urgency" factor. Will the customer wait for a special order, or will you lose "desired" sales if it isn't in stock? A "desired" sale is one that is profitable and occurs frequently enough to keep inventory turning (moving in and out).

Size and Location

Your store may be a kiosk in a mall's common area, one of many in a strip mall, a stand-alone storefront or a "store within a store."[1] Your store's size is an obvious factor in how much you can stock. Your store's location is your connection to the customer's you want to serve.

You'll need enough retail space to offer sufficient products and have ample inventory turns to reap a profit. The profit margin percentage on a medium-sized, well-stocked store in a busy strip mall may actually be comparable to that of smaller "store within a store" operation.

Larger isn't always better. You'll have a larger rent to cover, need more shelving and have a larger inventory investment. You'll need to know before you choose a location just how many egg timers or salt grinders you'll have to sell just to cover your overhead. You'll factor in overhead and employee costs and desired profit to determine the quantity you'll need to stock and sell.

You may decide that a smaller store is a better way to start. Just be sure to plan for growth. Don't let a five-year lease keep you from a better location.

[1] The store-within-a-store concept means that you would own and operate a "department" within an existing store. The storeowner would receive a percentage of your sales or would sublease space to you. This symbiotic relationship is actually common in the retail industry. For example, you might own the wine concession within a large kitchenware shop or the kitchen shop within a cooking school.

Goal-Setting

Now is the time to formalize your dream and set goals. You're probably already employed (or own another business), and you have a personal life—this means you'll be probably become sidetracked along the way to launching your retail gourmet store. Life can get in the way, but having set goals with completion dates will help you keep on track.

Creating Your Dream Store

Building your dream store in your head is an important first step to creating a profitable business. It will help you focus your energies and activities during the hectic days before you open. When decisions have to be made, do a mental check: Does this help my dream become a reality? Does it contribute to my goals?

Now let's talk about building a real business.

There are three ways to launch into business:

1. Start from scratch.
2. Invest in a franchise.
3. Buy an existing store.

All three starting methods can be the basis for a successful retail gourmet business.

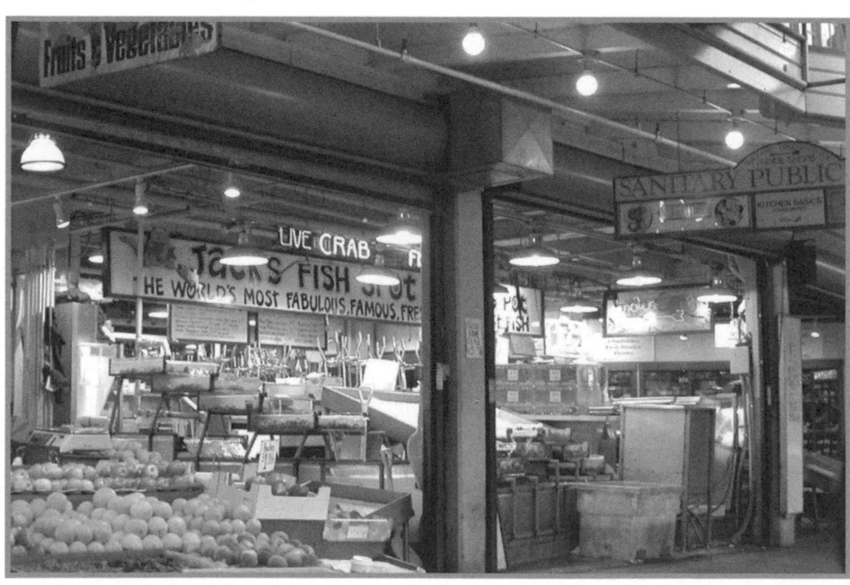

2

Launching Your Business

There are three ways to launch into business: 1) start from scratch, 2) invest in a franchise, or 3) buy an existing store. All three starting methods (scratch, franchise, existing) can be the basis for a successful retail gourmet business. The differences between each are as much emotional and psychological as they are financial. By weighing the pluses and minuses, factoring in your personality and business expectations and balancing it with your potential customers' needs and desires, you can decide the best method for your business.

Jump-Starting a Business

Purchasing an existing business can be the fastest way to get your doors open; however, it may not be the best choice for success. Remember, if the location is a poor one, the prior business had a bad reputation or the store's merchandise is overpriced, you may be hindering your potential. Availability is another factor when purchasing an existing business. The right business has to be on the market now or you have to make an offer that they cannot refuse.

Quality franchise organizations have market restrictions, assigned territories and other ways to keep their franchisees from competing or flooding the market. This may mean that your desired franchise is unavailable in your area. Popular franchises often require higher investments and a great personal net worth. When it comes to food-related businesses, franchises are most often of the fast-food variety, so your options are limited here.

Starting from Scratch

Starting your own retail store from the ground up gives you the opportunity to select every display shelf, put your own name on the door and create a fresh, new image—a business that most closely reflects your dream! However, the lengthy development and pre-opening period may stretch your patience and abilities (not to mention your pocketbook) beyond comfort levels.

When starting from scratch, you may be buying or building a storefront. This is the most costly investment and, unless you have a proven business track record in retail, can be a big risk. By leasing a unit in a retail mall or center, you'll have the infrastructure suitable for your store's needs without a significant investment.

What's the Best Way for Me?

If you have taken the time to do some personal reflection, compared your resources to your needs and set realistic expectations, you'll be better prepared to build, buy or lease your storefront, launch a new business and create a foundation for success and profits. The worksheet on pages 23 and 24 is a helpful assessment tool.

Don't Know the Answers?

If you don't know the pluses and minuses of the three ways to launch a business, you will find it helpful to immediately start researching your market, the competition and existing business opportunities. You'll have to do this before you prepare a formal business plan because the information you gather will help you prepare.

GOING INTO BUSINESS *(This form can be used to tally pluses and minuses, or to make comments.)*			
FACTORS	**FROM SCRATCH**	**FRANCHISE**	**BUY EXISTING BUSINESS**
Time			
Availability			
Launch Time *(Planning to opening)*			
Financial			
Cost			
Available Financing			
Investors			
Personal Worth Requirements			
Total Indebtedness			
Break-even Point			
Royalties and Fees			
Purchasing Restrictions			
Current Profitability			
Intangibles *(obstacles to success or existing profitability)*			
Goodwill			
Historical Recognition			
Known vs. Unknown			
Convenience			
Exclusivity			

GOING INTO BUSINESS

(This form can be used to tally pluses and minuses, or to make comments.)

FACTORS	FROM SCRATCH	FRANCHISE	BUY EXISTING BUSINESS
Assets			
Location			
Facility			
Equipment			
Existing Staff			
Customer Base			
Owner			
Independence			
Business Experience			
Food Experience			
Retail Experience			
Management Experience			
Owner Expectations			
Outside Expectations			
Training			
Support			
Marketshare			
Marketing Support			
Product Mix			
Competition			
Customer Needs			
Other *(your personal list)*			

3

The Basics of Buying a Gourmet Shop

Buying an existing retail gourmet store has its advantages and disadvantages. The prior store's track record of success can be a good reference point for your potential in the location. As with most retail businesses, location plays a vital role in your success. Before purchasing an existing business, carefully review all financial records, have appraisals done and, most importantly, consult a lawyer.

A great location significantly influences the cost of buying a business. However, the other potential benefits can make it your best route to having your own business.

- **Community recognition.** People already know they can find your "type" of store on that street.
- **Fewer building/construction issues.** Typically eliminates zoning, building-code compliance and construction licensing issues.
- **Restricted competition.** Shopping centers and strip malls

frequently have non-competitive agreements ensuring that you'll be the only cookware store in the complex.

This chapter addresses many of the issues that are important to you—the buyer. When it is your turn to become the seller, you'll benefit from understanding everyone's role in buying and selling your business. (We'll discuss both sides of the transaction here, and you'll learn more about selling your business in Chapter 22.)

Real Estate and Its Value

Real estate is the land itself and any permanent improvements made on the land, such as utility connections, parking lots, buildings, etc. The real property of a business is often its most valuable asset. However, many businesses are bought and sold without the real property being part of the sale because the business is operated in a leased building.

An experienced business broker and/or local real estate broker can guide you through determining the appropriate value for a business that includes real property. Income property values are frequently based on the potential future income to be derived from the property. The real estate value, then, is the present value of the estimated future net income, plus the present value of the estimated profit to be earned when the property is sold. This is the preferred approach when determining an accurate sales price for an income-producing property.

The Value of Other Assets

The business itself consists of everything the owner wishes to sell. Usually this means furniture, fixtures, equipment, leasehold improvements, etc. It may also include tax credits, favorable operating expenses, customer lists and name recognition.

The seller usually will set the sales price at the high end of this percentage, and the prospective buyer will set it at the low end. Don't assume that the seller is honest or upfront about asset values (or anything else for that matter). You don't want an adversarial relationship, but thoroughly check and recheck everything presented to you for accuracy.

Setting a sales price is not, of course, a straightforward process. Many factors need to be considered. Here are a few the seller might use:

Profitability

This has the most influence on sales price and salability of a retail business. The most common way to determine profitability is to examine the net operating income figure and compare this to industry standards and the regional standard for that type of operation.

Leasehold Terms and Conditions

The term remaining on the property lease and the monthly payment will greatly affect the sales price. Avoid anything less than a five-year lease unless it's very profitable, priced very low or you plan to relocate sooner based on growth. Most buyers also need a reasonable monthly payment and a reasonable common area maintenance payment.

Track Record

Businesses need to show acceptable track records to entice buyers. This usually means the business must be at least a year old. The track record will be used to project the business's future prospects. If a business depends on the work of highly skilled employees, such as a well-known pastry chef, this, too, can affect the price because it makes the business more difficult to expand and more expensive to operate.

Other Income

Most retail businesses don't earn significant income outside of store sales—usually less than 2 percent. However, there are rebates, interest on bank deposits, vending machines, salvage from aluminum and cardboard, etc.

Below-Market Financing

Often when a business is sold, the buyer puts up a small down payment and the seller then carries back the remainder of the sales price at favorable terms. Seller-financing is usually below market interest, and the buyer avoids the fees associated with bank loans.

Franchise Affiliation

If a retail store is part of a large franchise, the sales price will increase significantly. This is truer of the larger national franchises than the regional ones.

Selling Peaks

A seller should plan to market the business when there are as many potential buyers as possible. This means early spring and summer—especially if it's a store impacted by tourism—or after legislation limiting construction has passed, taxes are lowered, etc. Start your search during these peak sales periods.

Contingent Liabilities

Contingent liabilities reduce a business's net income. These may be coupons issued by the previous owner or pension plans that eat into your net profit margin. If a buyer cannot eliminate these expenses, they most likely represent a negative value that should be factored into the offering price.

Grandfather Clauses

New owners are expected to meet fire, health and safety codes that the previous owner may have been able to avoid because of being "grandfathered in" when regulations were passed. Grandfather clauses usually expire when a business changes hands. If this is the case, the seller or buyer may need to bring the building up to code. If the buyer is responsible for this, he or she will usually ask that the expense be deducted from the sales price. If the cost is very high, this could affect the salability of the business altogether.

Goodwill

The IRS determines goodwill as the amount of money paid for a business in excess of the current book value of the physical assets. Most investors, however, look at excess earnings as attributable to positive goodwill and deficient earnings to negative goodwill. A buyer may be willing to pay for goodwill, but a seller should expect the buyer to downplay its value in order to lower the sales price as much as possible.

Terms, Conditions and Price

In most cases, sellers will determine a likely sales price, terms and conditions, then pad those somewhat to create room for negotiation and compromise. Employing a skilled business broker can help you (the buyer) determine your offering price.

Terms

The terms of sale are the procedures used by the buyer to pay the seller. Seller-financing is a frequent arrangement where you will make a minimal down payment and pay the remainder over a 3- to 5-year period. All-cash offers are rare, so the seller probably won't be seeking that. It is in the seller's interest to seek a large down payment. Your financial advisor can assist you in determining how much down payment you should be willing to make. Sellers are also more likely to grant favorable terms to a buyer making a substantial down payment because the financial risk is lessened.

Conditions

There are several conditions the seller and buyer will attach to most sales contracts. Sometimes they are separate agreements, but most of the time they are part of the sales contract. The following lists conditions that are commonly addressed in business sales contracts. You'll need to determine what you will agree to that benefits you or "smoothes" the deal.

- **Conclusion of sale.** How long it will take to close the sale.

- **Buyer access.** Your access to the store and staff to facilitate a smooth transition.

- **Guarantees.** Sellers usually have to guarantee the condition of assets. Sometimes sellers have to guarantee that buyers can assume some of the business's current contracts. Imprecise language should also be avoided here. If the seller is making guarantees, then buying the relevant insurance to back up these claims is prudent.

- **Indemnification.** The conditions and penalty should anyone back out of the deal.

- **Escrow agent.** Agents hired to supervise the sales transaction paperwork. It is wise to use an independent third-party agent.
- **Legal requirements.** Agreement to comply with all pertinent laws and statutes.
- **Buyer's credit history.** Providing personal and business financial records and permission to run a credit report.
- **Security for seller-financing.** A clause requiring the seller's approval before the new owner can obtain additional financing. The promissory note will contain a default provision that the lender can foreclose if loan payments are not met, in addition to other specific provisions pertinent to the business.
- **Assumable loans and leases.** Detailing assumable contracts, loans and leases.
- **Life and disability insurance.** Insurance naming the seller as beneficiary should the buyer be unable to pay the loan due to death or disability.
- **Collection of receivables.** A fee paid to the seller if they collect receivables incurred by the seller but payable to the new owner.
- **Inventory sale.** A physical inventory of all resalable items and supplies taken at the end of escrow. Use an independent service and a separate bill of sale prepared for the agreed-upon price of this merchandise.
- **Non-compete clause.** An agreement that the seller will not open a competing business nearby. Usually a time period is set and "competing business" is defined.
- **Repurchase agreement.** Agreements that grant the seller an option to buy the business back within a certain time period.
- **Employment contract.** Details of a seller becoming an employee of the new owner.

- **Consulting contract.** An alternative to the employment contract. This may be a more acceptable employment contract that gives the new owner a tax-deductible expense but doesn't burden the former owner, either.

- **Conditions not met.** Detail if the seller can back out due to the buyer not meeting the sales conditions.

Initial Investment

You must estimate, as accurately as possible, the total initial investment needed to get your business up and running the way you envision it. Many businesses that could have been successful failed because they were undercapitalized. For exactly this reason, one of the very appealing aspects of purchasing an existing store is that many start-up costs are avoided. There are, however, a number of start-up costs even with transfer of ownership. Here are a few to be aware of:

- **Investigation costs.** Be willing to spend time and money to thoroughly examine the opportunities that are available.

- **Down payment.** A standard down payment is usually around a quarter of the sales price. The down payment can affect the sales price and, in many cases, sellers will accept a lower sales price with a larger down payment and vice versa.

- **Transaction costs.** Prorated insurance, payroll, property taxes, vacation pay, license renewal fees, advertising costs, etc., due on the close-of-escrow date.

- **Working capital.** Available cash to ensure sufficient supplies are on hand to run the store.

- **Deposits.** Cash deposits required of the new owner for utility, telephone, sales tax, payroll tax and lease deposits.

- **Licenses and permits.** All required operating licenses and permits for retail, health and occupational activities.

- **Legal fees.** Fees for legal advice, buyer negotiation and contract review.
- **Renovations.** Costs required to renovate or rectify building code violations.
- **Equipment and utensils.** Costs to purchase new or replacement equipment, supplies and displays. Don't forget to include maintenance agreements.
- **Advertising.** Costs to promote an opening or reopening, rebuild signage and offer promotional discounts and incentives.
- **Fictitious name registration.** Also know as "doing business as," or DBA. If the name of your store doesn't use your own name, the name usually must be registered at the local courthouse or County Recorder's Office.
- **Loan fees.** Loan fees from the lending parties.
- **Equity fees.** Attorney, document preparation and registration fees for selling common stock.
- **Insurance.** Lender-required life and disability insurance with the lender named as sole beneficiary. Adequate real property insurance may also be required.
- **Franchise fees.** Franchise transfer-of-ownership fee. This fee pays the franchiser for the costs of evaluating the new owner for the franchise. It is paid upfront and in cash before the new franchise can begin operations.
- **Distributorship fees.** Exclusive distributorship licenses or discontinuing a current license agreement may incur costs similar to franchise fees.
- **Pre-opening labor.** Labor required during pre-opening and transition period.

- **Accounting fees.** Fees for assistance in the evaluation of a business purchase.
- **Other consulting fees.** Fees for specialty services such as retail consultants, labor-relations specialists and computer consultants.
- **Other prepaid expenses.** Any prepayment required by a creditor.
- **Sales taxes.** Property subject to a transfer tax and supplies are often subject to sales or use tax.
- **Locksmith.** Cost to change all store locks after the sale is concluded.
- **Security.** Transfer or set-up fee for security service or systems.

The Biggest Cost of All

Contingency funds: You'll need enough working cash for at least the first six months' operating expenses. Among other things, it is often necessary to over-hire and over-schedule employees before an effective sales distribution pattern emerges. Most new business owners incur incredibly high expenses during the first six months of operation. Not having an ample contingency fund is the primary reason many businesses fail before they barely get started. You must also take into account your personal loss of income until the business can pay you a salary.

Strategies for Buying an Existing Gourmet Food Business

You must determine the type of retail operation that is right for you. Consider the store's investment yield, taxes and the effect the business will have on your personal life. Basically, buyers should be looking for a retail store that meets their financial requirements and that they are going to be happy working at day in and day out (including evenings).

Reviewing the Books

As a potential buyer, you must thoroughly analyze the finances of the store. Carefully study its current profitability and use this information to determine its potential for generating revenue.

It's a good idea to hire a skilled accountant to assist in determining whether the deal meets your investment requirements. Small Business Development Centers (SBDC) throughout the country offer free consulting services to businesses with fewer than 500 employees.

You should also complete at least a rough market and competition survey before performing the financial evaluation. This will ensure your familiarity with the store's location and will help you estimate future revenues and expenses. If you are unfamiliar with the area, an independent consulting service can provide a useful survey.

A seller expects a written offer with price, terms, conditions and an earnest money deposit before he or she will allow a potential buyer to review confidential financial information. It should be agreed that you could withdraw the offer if you're unhappy with the financial records; your earnest deposit is at risk unless the right to retract the offer is in place.

Evaluating the Merchandise

Your resale inventory is a retail store's biggest expense. As a potential buyer, you should take a random sample of cancelled invoices and check their consistency with sales and direct operating-supplies expenses listed on the current income statement. If these numbers match, you have a good idea of what product and supply expenses you will incur if no organizational and operational changes are made. The cancelled invoices are also a good test of the current owner's purchasing skills. If invoices show higher prices than those of competing suppliers, you can expect to decrease those expenses.

Purchasing Existing Inventory

Walking into the store, you can see the assortment of resale goods on hand. Don't overlook the back stock and warehoused inventory. Any store that has been operating for some time will have "dead" inventory—items that for one reason or another are not saleable. You should carefully review these items so you aren't paying full wholesale price for merchandise that should have been closed-out or tossed long ago.

Cash Budgets

Most lenders require that buyers prepare a cash budget. This will point out the operation's daily cash requirements and the times of year when short-term money must be borrowed to cover brief shortages.

You should analyze balance sheets and income statements. Balance sheets can reveal the anxiety level of a seller and indicate the management's ability. If this ability is in question, greater earnings may be possible under sound management. Income statements should be used to determine whether the store could have satisfied salary demands and provided a return on the initial investment, had it been under your management for the previous 12 months. As a buyer, you are basing your offer on current income, but purchasing the operation's future revenue-making ability.

Your Objectives

As a buyer, you must prioritize your objectives and consider the trade-offs that may be made to attain them. Buyers generally want to accomplish the following objectives:

- Best possible sales price
- Reasonable down payment
- Reasonable initial investment
- Maximum future profits

- Reduced possibility of failure
- Enhancement of borrowing power
- Minimizing tax liabilities

Financing

Your qualification for financing and the attainment of all necessary permits and licenses are the two most common obstacles to purchasing a business. There is little you, as a buyer, can do if you don't qualify for permits, unless you need to fix only simple code violations to qualify. In the financing realm, however, the seller and buyer have more control and can adjust the final sales contract to suit the buyer's needs. Buyers should beware that there is no bigger threat to their success than inadequate or inappropriate financing. Excessive debt burden is one of the most consistent reasons stores go under.

Equity Funds

Equity is capital that is at risk. Owners invest this money without any guarantee on a return. There are several types of equity financing techniques. The following are the most common:

- **Personal equity.** Funded entirely with personal equity or with a combination of personal equity and lease and debt financing.

- **Partnerships.** Partners investing together. These may be partners who participate in the business or "silent," inactive partners interested in a passive investment.

- **Corporations.** Raising capital through the sale of stock to private investors or the public.

- **Venture capital.** Professional investors or investment companies. Venture capitalists are interested in long-term financial gain and are less interested in the net operating profits of a new establishment. Buyers intending to purchase chain operations might be able to obtain venture capital because of the high earning potential.

Borrowing Money

It is often said that small-business owners have a difficult time borrowing money. This is not necessarily true. Banks make money by lending money. However, the inexperience of many small-business owners in financial matters often prompts banks to deny loan requests. Requesting a loan when you are not properly prepared sends a signal to your lender. That message is: High Risk!

To be successful in obtaining a loan, you must be prepared and organized. You must know exactly how much money you need, why you need it and how you will pay it back. You must be able to convince your lender that you are a good credit risk. Your loan request will be supported by your formal written business plan. (Chapter 5 discusses writing this important document.)

How Your Loan Request Will Be Reviewed

When reviewing a loan request, the lender is primarily concerned about repayment. To help determine your ability to repay, many loan officers will order a copy of your business credit report from a credit-reporting agency. Using the credit report and the information you have provided, the lending officer will consider the following issues:

- Have you invested savings or personal equity in your business totaling at least 25 to 50 percent of the loan you are requesting? (Remember, a lender or investor will not finance 100 percent of your business.)

- Do you have a sound record of credit-worthiness as indicated by your credit report, work history and letters of recommendation? This is very important.

- Do you have sufficient experience and training to operate a successful business?

- Have you prepared a loan proposal and business plan that

demonstrate your understanding of and commitment to the success of the business?

- Does the business have sufficient cash flow to make the monthly payments?

SBA Financial Programs

The Small Business Administration (SBA) offers a variety of financing options for small businesses. Whether you are looking for a long-term loan for machinery and equipment, a general working capital loan, a revolving line of credit or a micro-loan, the SBA has a financing program to fit your needs. These programs are discussed in detail on the SBA's Web site at www.sba.gov.

The 7(a) Loan Guaranty Program is the SBA's primary loan program. The SBA reduces risk to lenders by guaranteeing major portions of loans made to small businesses. This enables the lenders to provide financing to small businesses when funding is otherwise unavailable at reasonable terms. The eligibility requirements and credit criteria of the program are very broad in order to accommodate a wide range of financing needs.

There are also government-backed loan programs for minority- and women-owned businesses. You'll find links to these on the SBA site. For information on minority-owned business support, visit the Minority Business Development Association at www.mbda.gov.

In order to determine whether you qualify or whether an SBA business loan best suits your financing needs, contact your banker, one of the active SBA-guaranteed lenders or an SBA loan officer.

Friends and Relatives

Private sources such as friends and family willing to grant interest-free or low-interest loans. Beware of relying on family and friends for money. It is easy for feelings to become hurt and misunderstandings to damage relationships. Remember, you are risking your relationship along with their investment.

Banks and Credit Unions

The most common sources of funding are banks and credit unions. Loans are based on solid business proposals and your written business plan. Start by contacting the institute that handles your personal finances if you do not already have a business banker relationship.

Closing the Sale

Once you and the seller have agreed on the particulars, you will sign a binding sales contract and transfer ownership. There are often lawyers, brokers, accountants, lenders, escrow agents, government officials, trade unions, family members and other people involved in this transaction. It usually takes 30–60 days to finish the ownership transfer

According to the U.S. Department of Commerce, buying a franchise is the average person's most viable avenue to owning a business. Franchising can minimize your risk, it will enable you to start your business under a name and trademark that has already gained public acceptance and you will have access to training and management assistance from experienced people in the retail industry.

4

How to Invest in a Franchise

A franchise store can be an excellent way to have a dream business. According to the U.S. Department of Commerce, buying a franchise is the average person's most viable avenue to owning a business. You may want to consider such an investment. Franchising can minimize your risk, it will enable you to start your business under a name and trademark that has already gained public acceptance and you will have access to training and management assistance from experienced people in the retail industry. Oftentimes, you can obtain financial assistance; this allows you to start your business with less cash than you would ordinarily need.

On the other hand, you must make some sacrifices when entering a franchised operation. You lose a certain amount of control of the business. You will no longer truly be your own boss in some situations. You can be adversely affected by the actions of the franchiser (negative publicity, bankruptcy). Of course, you must pay a fee or share profits with the franchiser. This chapter will present some of the advantages and disadvantages of franchising and how to evaluate a franchise opportunity.

Franchise operations that offer specialty/gourmet food items range from Gloria Jean's Coffees to Ben & Jerry's Ice Cream to Honey Baked Ham Co.

to Incredibly Edible Delites Inc. (fruit/veggie "bouquets"). Most corporate Web sites will list general franchise information and provide you with contact information. There are also companies that specialize in helping potential franchisees locate and set up a franchise outlet. Simply search the Web for "franchise opportunities," "food franchises" and "franchise support" to find specifics.

Definition of Franchising

Essentially, franchising is a plan of distribution under which an individually owned business is operated as though it were a part of a large chain. Products are standardized. Standardized trademarks, symbols, design elements and equipment are used. A supplier (the franchiser) gives the individual dealer (the franchisee) the right to sell, distribute and market the franchiser's product by using the franchiser's name, reputation and selling techniques.

The franchise agreement (or contract) usually grants the franchisee the exclusive right to sell, or otherwise represent the franchiser, in a specified geographic location. In return for this exclusive right, the franchisee agrees to pay a sum of money (a franchise fee) or a percentage of gross sales and/or to buy equipment or supplies from the franchiser—often these options are variously combined.

Advantages of Franchising

As a franchisee, you have the luxury of starting a business with:

- **Limited experience.** You are taking advantage of the franchiser's experience; experience that you probably would have gained the hard way—through trial and error.

- **Reduced capital outlay and a strengthened financial/credit standing.** Some franchisers provide financial assistance to establish your retail with less than the usual cash investment. With the name of a well-known, successful franchiser behind you, your standing with financial institutions can also be strengthened. For example, the franchiser may accept a down payment with your note for the balance of the needed capital. Or, the franchiser may allow you to delay in making payments on royalties or other fees in order to help you through the "rough spots."

- **Well-developed image and consumer recognition of proven products and services.** The goods and services of the franchiser are typically proven and widely known. Therefore, your business has "instant" pulling power. To develop such pulling power on your own might take years of promotion and considerable investment.

- **Competently designed facilities, layout, displays and fixtures.** The franchising company has designed standardized facilities, layouts, displays and fixtures based upon their experience with many dealers.

- **Chain buying power.** You may receive savings through chain-style purchasing of products, equipment, supplies, advertising materials and other business needs.

- **Business training and support.** The franchisee's training program and ongoing business development support system teaches you proven business methods and gives you a valuable safety net. You can normally expect to be trained in the mechanics of the retail business and guided in its day-to-day operation until you are proficient at the job. Management consulting services should be provided by the franchiser on a continuing basis. This often includes help with recordkeeping as well as other accounting assistance. Remember, your success (and potential failure) directly reflects on their corporate image.

- **National or regional promotion and publicity.** The national or regional promotion of the franchiser will help your business. In addition, you will receive help and guidance with local advertising. The franchiser's program of research and development will assist you in keeping up with competition and changing times.

All of these factors can help increase your income and lower your risk of failure.

Disadvantages of Franchising

There are also disadvantes of franchsing. Be sure to wiegh them carefully.

- **Submission to imposed standardized operations.** You cannot make all the rules. Contrary to the "be your own boss" lures in franchise advertisements, you may not be your only boss. In addition, you must subjugate your personal identity to the name of the franchiser. Obviously, if you would like your operation to be known by your own name, a franchise is not for you. The franchiser exerts fundamental control and obligates you to:
  - Conform to standardized procedure.
  - Handle specific products or services that may not be particularly profitable in your marketing area.
  - Follow other policies that may benefit others in the chain but not you. This means that you forfeit the freedom to make many decisions—to be your own boss.
- **Sharing of profits with the franchiser.** The franchiser nearly always charges a royalty (a percentage of gross sales). Frequently, this royalty fee must be paid whether the franchisee makes a profit or not. Sometimes such fees are exorbitantly out of proportion to the profit.
- **Required purchases.** Merchandise, supplies or equipment that the franchiser requires you to buy from the corporation might be obtained elsewhere for less. A federal government study showed that in food franchising, many franchisees that were required to buy a large proportion of supplies from their franchisers were paying higher prices than they could obtain on their own. Additionally, you might pay more to the franchiser than other franchisees for the same services.
- **Lack of freedom to meet local competition.** Under a franchise agreement, you may be restricted in establishing selling prices, in introducing additional products or services or dropping unprofitable

ones, even in the face of insidious local competition.

- **Danger of contracts being slanted to the advantage of the franchiser.** Clauses in some contracts imposed by the franchiser provide for unreasonably high sales quotas, mandatory working hours, cancellation or termination of the franchise for minor infringements and/or restrictions on the franchisee in transferring the franchise or recovering the investment. The territory assigned the franchisee may overlap with that of another franchisee or may be otherwise inequitable. In settling disputes of any kind, the bargaining power of the franchiser is usually greater.

- **Time consumed in preparing reports required by the franchiser.** Franchisers require specific reports. The time and effort necessary to prepare these may be inordinately burdensome. On the other hand, you should recognize that if these reports were helpful to the franchiser, they probably would help you to manage your business more effectively.

- **Sharing the burden of the franchiser's faults.** While ordinarily the franchiser's chain will have developed goodwill among consumers, there may be instances in which ill will has been developed. For example, if a customer received poor service in one outlet, he or she is apt to become disgruntled with the whole chain. As one outlet in the chain, you will suffer regardless of the excellence of your particular unit. Furthermore, the franchiser may fail. You must bear the brunt of the chain's mistakes as well as share the glory of its good performances.

Minority Participation in Franchising

A number of franchise systems have developed special programs for minority individuals who seek to go into business for themselves. One such program asks the minority individual for only a 2 percent down payment. The franchiser matches this with 98 percent financing and up to a year of training.

Another program is a joint venture between a minority-owned business and an established franchising company. This joint venture is not a merger of the two companies; it is a plan whereby each company contributes an equal amount of dollars, but all responsibility for day-to-day operations is left with the minority-owned company.

Franchise Financing

There are a growing number of alternatives for individuals and investors who want to enter franchising or expand their current market position. More and more local and regional banks, along with national non-bank lenders, are offering franchise financing. These lending institutions have a greater appreciation for the importance of franchising in the marketplace, for its future growth and stability as a distribution method. For example, the International Franchise Association (www.franchise.org) lists more than 30 bank and non-bank franchise lenders in its Franchise Opportunities Guide this year. The U.S. Small Business Administration (www.sba.gov), which has recently backed more than 60,000 small-business loans totaling over $14 billion, works with local and regional banks to offer its guaranteed loan program to start-up franchisees.

Evaluating a Franchise Opportunity

A franchise costs money. One can be purchased for as little as a few hundred dollars or as much as a quarter of a million dollars or more. Hence, it is vital that you investigate and evaluate carefully any franchise before you invest.

Beware of the "fast buck" artists and poorly executed franchise programs. The popularity of franchising has attracted an unsavory group of operators who will take you if they can. Sometimes known as "front-money men," they usually offer nothing more than the sale of equipment and a catchy business name. Once they sell you the equipment, they do not care whether you succeed or fail. If you are promised tremendous profits in a short period, be wary. Other franchisers aren't unscrupulous but merely have poor or fiscally unsound business practices.

Franchise Research

To learn more about franchising and food-related retail franchise opportunities, check out the consulting, government and association Web sites listed below.

- A Consumer Guide to Buying a Franchise—www.consumer-guides .info/business/franchises
- Federal Trade Commission—www.ftc.gov/bcp/franchise/netfran .htm
- International Franchise Association—www.franchise.org
- Wall Street Journal's Startup Journal—www.startupjournal.com
- Food Franchise.com—www.foodfranchise.com
- Findlaw—caveats on investing in franchises—www.biz.findlaw.com /bookshelf/sblg/SBLGCHP6.html
- BISON.com—franchise advice—www.bison1.com

Conclusion

Without franchising, it is doubtful that thousands of small-business investors could ever have started. The system permits goods to be marketed by a small-business owner in a way that otherwise can be done only with the vast sums of money and number of managerial people possessed by large corporations. As a new owner, you can draw from the experience and resources—promotional, managerial, educational and research—of a large, established parent company.

Unfortunately, not even the help of a good franchiser can guarantee success.

You will still be primarily responsible for the success or failure of your venture. As in any other type of business, your return will be directly related to the amount and effectiveness of your investment in time and money.

5

Planning for Success—Writing a Business Plan

No one plans to fail—but you can plan for success. Creating a formal written business plan is an absolute necessity if you are seeking outside financing. However, its greatest benefit may be as your personal road map to success. Many entrepreneurs breeze by this step in creating their business. This is a mistake. Yes, we know that it is hard and boring and seems like busy work, but if you cannot tackle this, how will you be prepared for paperwork, tax forms, profit and loss statements, government forms and other similar business requirements?

Those who plan ahead are prepared for the ups and downs of owning a business, and they are better prepared to deal with the unexpected. Unless you have a crystal ball, you cannot see the future, but you can have the information and tools necessary to make wise choices for yourself, your employees and your business.

To move beyond a dream, you must have a plan that will:

- Help you clarify your ideas and dreams.

- Share your dream with family and friends (especially if they are going to be financial backers or silent partners).
- Focus your attention on building a solid business foundation.
- Prepare you for potential obstacles and pitfalls.
- Give you a reality-check. Are you suited to the hours? Can you afford that fancy storefront? Does hiring employees scare you? Are you prepared for the impact it will have on your family life?
- Chart your path to success. What will you sell? Who will buy it? What profits can you expect?
- Benchmark your business. Did you meet your budgets? Are your assumptions valid, or do they need to be updated based on new information? What worked? What didn't work? What should you do differently?

Five Keys of Success

Before you can write anything down, you need to do some research within your community. You'll need to know whether you'll have all five of the keys of success.

1. **Need.** Does your community need another retail store such as yours? Is there a niche that is underserved?
2. **Customers.** Are there enough potential customers interested in your products to make you profitable? Will you have to spend heavily on advertising to reach them? Can they afford your products?
3. **Location.** Can your business be conveniently located? Can you afford the location? Are you near your ideal customer?
4. **Products.** Can you offer what your customers want at the price they will pay? Do you know what they want?

5. **Service.** Can you set your business apart from your competitors and make it worth the trip? Can you afford sufficient staffing?

Some of the answers to the above questions will require some research. We'll discuss each point in the order in which it would appear in your business plan.

What a Business Plan Includes

What goes in a business plan? Your business plan can be divided into four distinct sections: 1) the description of the business, 2) the marketing plan, 3) the management plan, and 4) the financial management plan. Addenda to the business plan should include the executive summary, supporting documents and financial projections.

A Sample Business Plan Outline

Use the outline below as a guide to creating your first business plan. Throughout your first year and beyond, you should review and update your plan. Think about your short- and long-term goals; include what you've learned about your customers, your competitors and how to keep your business growing.

Elements of a Business Plan

I. Cover sheet
II. Statement of purpose
III. Table of contents

A. The Business

1. Description of business
2. Marketing
3. Competition
4. Operating procedures
5. Personnel

6. Business insurance
7. Financial data

B. Financial Data

1. Loan applications
2. Capital equipment and supply list
3. Balance sheet
4. Break-even analysis
5. Pro-forma income projections (profit and loss statements)
   a. Three-year summary
   b. Detail by month, first year
   c. Detail by quarters, second and third years
   d. Assumptions upon which projections were based
6. Pro-forma cash flow
   a. Follow guidelines for number 5

C. Supporting Documents

1. Tax returns of principals for last three years
2. Personal financial statement (all banks have these forms)
3. Copy of proposed lease or purchase agreement for building space
4. Copy of licenses and other legal documents
5. Copy of resumes of all principals
6. Copies of letters of intent from suppliers, etc.

Business Description

In this section, provide a detailed description of your business. An excellent question to ask yourself is "What business do I want to be in?" In answering this question, include your products, services and customer market as well as a thorough description of what makes your store unique.

Remember that as you develop your business plan and learn new facts, you may have to modify or revise your initial answers. The process of researching and writing your business plan has another potential benefit: What you learn may save you from losing your life savings and risking your financial future. Look honestly at your business concept's potential, your personal potential for success and what it will take to make it profitable.

The business description section is divided into three primary sections: Section 1 describes your business; Section 2, the product or service you will be offering; and Section 3, the location of your business and why this location is desirable (if you have a franchise, some franchisers will assist in site selection). The description of your business should clearly identify goals and objectives and it should clarify why you are, or why you want to be, in business.

When describing your business, you should explain:

- **Legalities.** Business form: proprietorship, partnership or corporation. What licenses or permits you will need.

- **Business description.** Twenty-five words or less describing the business. An example would be: An upscale retail specialty store offering the latest cookware, accessories and gourmet cheeses.
    - Memorize this quick pitch; you'll use it often with potential vendors and suppliers, bankers, lenders and friends. Businesses aren't launched by the efforts of one person. Let people in on your dream and you'll find plenty of help.

- **What your product or service is.** Perhaps a sample "daily offering" list could be included.

- **Business type.** Is it a new, independent business, a takeover, an expansion, a franchise?

- **Why your business will be profitable.** What are the growth opportunities? Will franchising negatively impact your growth opportunities?

- **When your business will be open.** What days? hours?

- **What you have learned about your kind of business from outside sources** (trade suppliers, bankers, other franchise owners, franchiser, publications).

A cover sheet will precede the description. It should include the name, address and telephone number of the business and the names of all principals.

In the description of your business, describe the unique aspects and how or why they will appeal to consumers. Emphasize any special features that you feel will appeal to customers and explain how and why these features are appealing.

Legal Forms of Business

When organizing a new business, one of the most important decisions is choosing the structure of the business. Your attorney and accountant can provide you with the legal and financial advantages and disadvantages of each. Factors influencing your decision about your business organization include:

- Legal restrictions.
- Liabilities assumed.
- Type of business operation.
- Earnings distribution.
- Capital needs.
- Number of employees.
- Tax advantages or disadvantages.
- Length of business operation.

Below you will find a brief description of the business entities you can choose.

- **Sole proprietorship.** The easiest and least costly way of starting a business. A sole proprietorship can be formed by simply finding a location and opening the door for business. Start-up attorney's fees will be less than those of other business forms. The owner has absolute authority over all business decisions. The biggest negative to a sole proprietorship is your personal liability should the business default on a loan or be involved in a legal dispute.

- **Partnership.** Two or more parties that join together to share ownership. The two most common partnership types are general and limited. A general partnership can be formed simply by an oral agreement between two or more persons, but a legal partnership agreement drawn up by an attorney is highly recommended. Legal fees for drawing up a partnership agreement are higher than those for a sole proprietorship, but may be lower than incorporating. A partnership agreement could be helpful in solving any disputes. However, partners are responsible for the other partner's business actions, as well as their own.

- **Corporation.** A business entity where control depends upon stock ownership. A business may incorporate without an attorney, but legal advice is highly recommended. The corporate structure is usually the most complex and is more costly to organize. Control depends on stock ownership. Persons with the largest stock ownership control the corporation, not the total number of shareholders. Small, closely held corporations can operate more informally, but recordkeeping cannot be eliminated. Officers of a corporation can be liable to stockholders for improper actions. Liability is generally limited to stock ownership, except where fraud is involved. You may want to incorporate as a "C" or "S" corporation.

- **Limited liability company (LLC).** An LLC is not a corporation, but it offers many of the same advantages. Many small-business owners and entrepreneurs prefer an LLC because they combine the limited liability protection of a corporation with the "pass through" taxation of a sole proprietorship or partnership. An LLC has advantages over corporations that allow greater flexibility in management and business organization.

Products/Services

Here is where you'll describe the benefits of your goods and services from your customers' perspective. Successful business owners must have a good idea of what their customers want or expect from them. This type of anticipation can be helpful in building customer satisfaction and loyalty. Additionally, it is a wise strategy for beating the competition or retaining your competitive advantage.

Describe:

- What you are selling. Include your retail products and ready-to-eat offerings (if appropriate) here.

- How your product or service will benefit the customer.

- Which products/services are in demand.

- What is different about the product or service your business is offering. In marketing, this is called your USP (Unique Selling Position) and should be at the center of your marketing message.

The Location

The location of your business can play a decisive role in its success or failure. Remember the old maxim, "Location, location, location." Your location should be for your customers' convenience, it should be accessible and it should provide a sense of comfort and security.

In your business plan, you'll be explaining why your potential location is a wise decision for your business. If you are building or purchasing a building, you would also include construction and renovation expectations here.

Consider these questions when addressing this section of your business plan:

- What are your location needs?
- What kind of space will you need? Is there room to expand?
- Are there environmental or zoning issues to be considered?
- Why is the area desirable? the building desirable?
- Is it easily accessible?
- Is street lighting adequate?
- Is it affordable?

Think About Joining In

Notice how there seems to be a fast food store on every corner. This isn't poor planning but a belief that dining and shopping means being within reach when the urge strikes. Being located near a green grocer, a fish market or a gourmet restaurant brings specific types of customers to your local.

Location = Customers

After selecting various potential retail sites or when assessing existing retail stores for sale, be sure to obtain as many lifestyle and demographic facts as you can about each.

- How many gourmet food or upscale food-related stores are located in the area?
  - Are there upscale full-service markets or other stores that also carry these items in your area?
  - Will you be a direct or indirect competitor? A direct competitor is a retail store that carries the same inventory. An indirect competitor is one that carries similar goods.
- Can you find out something about their sales volume?
- Since gourmet stores typically attract primarily local inhabitants:
  - What is the population of the area?
  - Is the trend of population increasing, stationary or declining?
  - Are the people native-born, mixed or chiefly foreign? This information can help you stock appropriate ethnic food items.
  - What do they do for a living? Are they predominantly laborers, clerks, executives or retired persons? Are they of all ages or principally old, middle-aged or young?
- To help you gauge your potential customers' buying power, find out:

    - The average sales price and rental rates for homes in the area.
    - Their per-capita income.
    - Average family size.

- Is the building/location suitable for a retail establishment? If you are serving any ready-to-eat food that may require specific zoning permits, does it meet health department standards? Available parking and visibility from the street are also important factors to consider.

The Marketing Plan

Marketing plays a vital role in successful business ventures. How well you market your business, along with a few other considerations, will ultimately determine your degree of success or failure. The key element of a successful marketing plan is to know your customers: their likes, dislikes and expectations. By identifying these factors, you can develop a marketing strategy that will allow you to arouse and fulfill their needs.

Who Are Your Customers?

As we discussed earlier, identify your customers by their age, sex, income/educational level and residence. At first, target only those customers who are most likely to purchase your product or service. When you are ready to expand your business, consider modifying the marketing plan to include other potential customers. These customers may cost more to acquire, but you'll be developing a new customer base and a lasting business.

Customer Demographic Research

Demographic information isn't just boring statistics. It's the numerical story of your community and customer base. Gourmet (food and preparation products) retailers appeal to a specific economic group and within that group there are other groups defined by sex, age, family relationships, marital status and employment categories.

Your local chamber of commerce, state business development agency, retail associations and peers can assist you with demographics (economic and lifestyle patterns) of your community and business research.

Visit your local library or online databanks for additional data. At the library (ask about free research assistance from trained librarians), check out the following resources:

- Demographics USA (ZIP edition)—market statistics.
- Standard Rate & Data Service—look under "gourmet cooking/fine foods" and cross-reference "market," "lifestyle" and "consumer."
- Standard & Poor's Industry Surveys.

Visit these government and demographic research sites:

- www.ameristat.org
- www.quickfacts.census.gov/qfd/index.html
- www.searchbug.com/reference/demographics.asp

Your marketing plan should be included in your business plan and contain answers to the questions outlined below. Depending upon your market and your store profile, you may have other questions that you need to address in your marketing plan.

- Who are your customers? Define your target market(s).
- Are your markets (potential customer base) growing? steady? declining?
- Is your market share growing? steady? declining?
- If a franchise, how is your market segmented?

- Are your markets large enough to expand?

- How will you attract, hold and increase your market share? How will you promote your business?

- If a franchise, will the franchiser provide assistance in this area?

- What pricing strategy have you devised (we'll discuss pricing in greater detail later in this chapter)?
    - Price can be an important purchasing factor. However, for upscale buyers, it isn't their primary concern.

    - Low prices aren't always the right pricing strategy. Focus on value and service.

    - Remember, every grocery store in America sells salt, but you sell more than a seasoning—you sell unique types of salt, creative packaging and reputations.

Competition

An important part of determining your store's potential success is to study the competition. Finding your competitive edge or discovering a niche market is important. Learning what others are successful with can be helpful. In every business, keeping in tune to the competition is how you set yourself apart.

Questions like these can help you:

- Who are your five nearest direct competitors?
- Who are your five nearest indirect competitors?
- How are their businesses: steady? increasing? decreasing?
- What have you learned from their operations? from their advertising?
- What are their strengths and weaknesses?
- How do their products or service differ from yours?

Start a file on each of your competitors. Keep manila envelopes of their advertising and promotional materials and their pricing strategy techniques.

Review these files periodically, determining when and how often they advertise, sponsor promotions and offer sales. Study the copy used in the advertising and promotional materials, and their sales strategy. For example, is their copy short? descriptive? catchy? How much do they reduce prices for sales? Using this technique can help you to better understand your competitors and how they operate their businesses.

Scouting the Competition

We've outlined some suggestions below to help you scout the competition. Remember, these are research expeditions to help you create your store's niche, learn from their experiences and determine your potential for success.

- **Mark your potential location on a street map.** Draw a circle around the mark: for "walking" neighborhoods, a six-block radius should be enough, and for "driving" neighborhoods, start with a quarter-mile. This is your initial study area. You can always expand your research territory based on how far you believe people will travel for your products.

- **Visit every business that sells similar items (no matter what the quality level or brand), including grocery stores.** These are your competitors. Even if they aren't a gourmet retailer, they are competing for your customers' attention and dollars.

- **Be a critic.** Make notes of what works and what doesn't.

- **How do the patrons interact with the physical surroundings?** Are the lines confusing during peak hours? Are the displays attractive? Are their any items you think are missing from their offerings?

- **Visit during peak hours.** Look at who is shopping there and what they are buying.

What Will You Sell to Customers?

What you offer your customers every day (supplemented with seasonal offerings) is called your product mix. Beyond upscale food ingredients, tasty tidbits and food prep equipment, you may choose to have other "profit centers," such as serving high tea, gourmet coffee by the pound or ice cream by the scoop. (Chapter 11 also discusses various food and non-food items that can comprise your resale inventory, how to satisfy customer demands and how to focus on the profit-makers.)

In your business plan, you'll discuss what products you will be offering, why you feel these are your best choices for potential customers and why they will buy them. You should back up all your assumptions with local and national data from your research. Report on trends, seasonal additions, brand name recognition and anticipated product category growth.

Pricing

Your pricing strategy is another marketing technique you can use to improve your overall competitiveness. Get a feel for the pricing strategy your competitors are using. That way you can determine if your prices are in line with competitors in your market area and if they are in line with industry averages.

Your retail "style" and customer demographics are factors. Are you a family friendly store with comfort foods? Are your customers "foodies," seeking serving pieces for an elegant presentation or imported caviar? Are your customers interested in natural or organic products? Do your products appeal to the discriminating buyers who read *Gourmet* and *Bon Appétit*?

Some of the pricing considerations are:

- **Delivered costs.** Consumers understand that imported goods, the top brand names, fresh and organic ingredients and specialty items cost more than possible mass-market "equivalents."

- **Competitive position.** Exclusivity can be a plus if you are marketing to the crowd that relates to that. However, a more competitive position may appear to a broader range of people within your community. If you are located in a busy area with lots of gourmet resources, your pricing should be competitive without undercutting your perceived value.

- **Pricing below competition.** Undercutting the competition can bring people in, but it is quality and value that keeps them. Besides, gourmet equals cost in most minds. If your customer demographics are at the upper end for your community, pricing isn't the deciding factor in purchasing. In fact, it can have the opposite effect. You'll find pushing exclusivity, vanity, competitiveness and style are more important.

- **Pricing above competition.** By definition, gourmet shops are already priced above "traditional" retailers that offer similar, yet less exclusive or lower-quality products. Pricing yourself above other gourmet retail shops may work in some instances. Some products are more, some are less, but with the emphasis on quality, your customers won't be worrying about a few cents here or there.

- **Multiple pricing.** Offer multiple-buy discounts to increase sales per customer. This pricing concept works best with things like cookbooks (buy 1, get 1 at 25% off), table linens (buy 6 napkins, get 2 free) and items that come in multiple flavors, colors or typically used by groups.

- **Service components.** If you offer any type of ready-to-eat food that requires service, your pricing must cover additional service staff. Other hands-on services, such as gift shoppers, personal shoppers (to outfit new kitchens) and other time/labor-intensive extras, will need to be factored in.

- **Overhead costs.** Don't let your facility costs escalate your product pricing unreasonably. Sure, it's great to be located in the new strip mall, but how many $4.95 kitchen tools will you have to sell every month just to meet expenses?

Advertising and Public Relations

How you advertise and promote your store can make or break your business. Having good products and excellent service without advertising is like not having a business at all. Often retail store owners operate under the mistaken concept that people will just drop by on their own, and channel money that should be used for advertising and promotions to other areas of the business. While location is important, unless they open up the door and come in, it doesn't help much. Advertising and promotions are the lifeline of a business and should be treated as such. (See Chapters 9 and 10 on marketing your store.)

- Devise a plan that uses advertising and networking as a means to promote your business.
- Develop short, descriptive copy (text material) that clearly identifies your goods or services, location and price (remember, price isn't always the deciding factor so this isn't always important).
- Use catchy phrases to arouse the interest of your readers, listeners or viewers.
- Make their mouths water! Don't just tell people what you sell—tell them why they should buy from you.

In the case of a franchise, the franchiser will provide advertising and promotional materials as part of the franchise package; you may need approval to use any materials that you and your staff develop. Whether or not this is the case, as a courtesy, allow the franchiser the opportunity to review, comment on and, if required, approve these materials before using them. Make sure the advertisements you create are consistent with the image the franchiser is trying to project.

Your marketing plan section should include the various advertising and public relations efforts you will employ (how you will reach potential customers) and the estimated cost of the campaigns. Assign percentages of your annual budget to the various media you will use. Don't forget to list any co-op advertising dollars you anticipate receiving from manufacturers and suppliers. Other advertising efforts that should be included in your marketing plan are phone directories, roadside signs, discount coupons, frequent-buyer programs, point-of-sale displays, samples and your open house.

Remember, the more care and attention you devote to your marketing program, the more successful your business will be.

The Management Plan

Managing a business requires more than just the desire to be your own boss. It demands dedication, persistence, the ability to make decisions and the ability to manage both employees and finances. Your management plan, along with your marketing and financial management plans, sets the foundation for and facilitates the success of your business.

Like a building and your store's merchandise, people are resources—they are the most valuable assets a business has. You will soon discover that your staff will play an important role in the total operation of your business. Consequently, it's imperative that you know what skills you do and do not possess since you will have to hire personnel to supply the skills you lack. Even if you can create a profit and loss statement or design a Web page, you need to consider if working on these tasks are the best use of your time. Until there are more than 24 hours in a day, you'll need to prioritize your activities so those tasks that earn money come first. So don't be afraid to hire someone to do the general operations work.

Your management plan should answer questions such as:

- How does your background/business experience help you in this business?
- What are your weaknesses and how can you compensate for them?
- Who will be on the management team?
- What are their strengths/weaknesses?
- What are their duties?

- Are these duties clearly defined?
- If a franchise, what type of assistance can you expect from the franchiser?
- Will this assistance be ongoing?
- What are your current personnel needs?
- What are your plans for hiring and training personnel?
- What salaries, vacations and holidays will you offer?
- If a franchise, are these issues covered in the management package the franchiser will provide?
- What benefits, if any, can you afford at this point?

If this is a franchise, the operating procedures, manuals and materials devised by the franchiser should be included in this section of the business plan. Lenders will consider the strength of the franchiser as part of your management capabilities. Study these documents carefully when writing your business plan and be sure to incorporate the important highlights. The franchiser should assist you with managing your franchise. Take advantage of their expertise and develop a management plan that will ensure the success for your franchise and satisfy the needs and expectations of employees as well as those of the franchiser.

The Financial Management Plan

Sound financial management is one of the best ways for your business to remain profitable and solvent. How well you manage the finances of your business is the cornerstone of every successful business venture. Each year thousands of potentially successful businesses fail because of poor financial management. As a business owner, you will need to identify and implement policies that will lead to and ensure that you will meet your financial obligations.

To effectively manage your finances, plan a sound, realistic budget by determining the actual amount of money needed to open your business (start-up costs) and the amount needed to keep it open (operating costs). The first step to building a sound financial plan is to devise a start-up budget. Your start-up budget will usually include such one-time-only costs as major equipment, utility deposits, down payments, etc.

Operating Budget

An operating budget is prepared when you are actually ready to open for business. The operating budget will reflect your priorities in terms of how you spend your money, the expenses you will incur and how you will meet those expenses (income). Your operating budget also should include money to cover the first six to nine months of operation. (For more information on operating budgets, see Chapter 19.)

The financial section of your business plan should include any loan applications you've filed, your capital equipment and supply list, balance sheet, break-even analysis, pro-forma income projections (profit and loss statement) and pro-forma cash flow. The income statement and cash flow projections should include a three-year summary (detail by month for the first year; then by quarter for the second and third years).

Developing projections is probably the most difficult aspect of writing your business plan. You should strive to be as accurate as possible based upon your research. Overstating your sales in hopes of impressing lenders or investors can backfire on you should you not reach these estimates. Understating your sales can mean that you won't be prepared to satisfy the demand.

The accounting system and the inventory-control system that you will be using are generally addressed in this section of the business plan. (Chapter 12 discusses computerized accounting and inventory systems.)

If a franchise, the franchiser may stipulate in the franchise contract the type of accounting and inventory systems you may use. If this is the case, he or she should have a system already intact and you will be required to adopt this system. Whether you develop the accounting and inventory systems yourself, have an outside financial advisor develop the systems or the franchiser provides these systems, you will need to acquire a thorough understanding of each segment and how it operates. Your financial advisor can assist you in developing this section of your business plan.

The following questions should help you determine the amount of start-up capital you will need to purchase and open a franchise.

- How much money do you have?
- How much money will you need to purchase the franchise?
- How much money will you need for start-up?
- How much money will you need to stay in business?

Other questions that you will need to consider are:

- What are your sales and profit goals for the coming year?

- If a franchise, will the franchiser establish your sales and profit goals? Will they expect you to reach and retain a certain sales level and profit margin?

- What financial projections will you need to include in your business plan?

- What kind of inventory-control system will you use?

Your plan should include an explanation of all projections. Unless you are thoroughly familiar with financial statements, get help in preparing your cash flow and income statements and your balance sheet. Your aim is not to become a financial wizard, but to understand the financial tools well enough to gain their benefits. Your accountant or financial advisor can help you accomplish this goal.

Business Plan Resources

Business experts recommend that you write your own business plan as the process is as important as the finished plan. There are numerous Web resources (search for "retail business plan") to help you write a plan for internal and external purposes.

- Purchase a fill-in-the-blank business plan book from your local bookstore or a popular software package like Business Plan Pro from Palo Alto Software to get you started. Business Plan Pro includes a sample retail store business plan. These guides will ask thought-provoking questions and help you organize your thoughts, gather research data and present it in a straightforward manner.

- Check with your state's Small Business Development Center, the Small Business Administration (SBA) at www.sba.gov or your local university for free or low-cost business plan writing classes. Besides learning how to write your plan, the discipline of attending a class can provide focus for busy entrepreneurs.

- Hire a business communications specialist to "spruce up" your plan. An experienced business plan writer can polish your presentation to dazzle bankers and investors.

- Review free sample business plans at BPlans.com (www.bplans .com).

Before engaging in any business activity, your first step should be to seek the guidance of a lawyer. You will undoubtedly have many legal questions, and you will need legal counseling during the opening period. The services of a local accountant should also be retained. Your accountant will be instrumental in setting up the business and can provide you with vital financial advice.

6

Launching Your Business—Pre-Opening Activities

Each store launch has its own unique and challenging problems. Once you have determined your desired opening date, you'll have plenty of pre-opening tasks to accomplish. Before engaging in any business activity, your first step should be to seek the guidance of a lawyer. You will undoubtedly have many legal questions and you will need legal counseling during the opening period. The services of a local accountant should also be retained. Your accountant will be instrumental in setting up the business and can provide you with vital financial advice.

Laws, Regulations and Licenses

Determine your state's requirements for starting a business as early as possible. A good place to start is your state's Secretary of State or Business Development Office Web site. All states have different regulations so don't assume anything.

There is generally a fee required for registering a new business. You will need to confirm that no other businesses are currently using your particular business name and file assumed business name applications, if required.

If your state has an income tax on wages, request all pertinent information from the State Department of Labor or Taxation. This would include all required forms, tax tables and tax guides. Also, contact the State Department of Wage and Hour for their employee/employer regulations.

City Business License

Almost all cities and most counties require a permit to operate a business. Contact your local city hall for licensing information. Your application will be checked by the zoning board to make certain that the business conforms to all local regulations. Purchasing an existing retail store will eliminate most of these clearances.

Sales Tax

Contact the State Revenue or Taxation Agency concerning registry and collection procedures. Each state has its own methods of taxation on the sale of food products. Most states that require collection on food and beverage sales also require an advance deposit or bond against future taxes to be collected.

Sales tax is collected on the retail price paid by the end user. You must present the wholesaler/distributor with your sales tax permit information when placing orders and sign a tax release card for their files. Make certain that you comply with your state's regulations or you may be required to pay a use tax.

Certain counties and/or cities may also assess an additional sales tax in addition to the state sales tax. This entire issue needs to be thoroughly researched, as an audit in the future could present you with a considerable tax liability.

Health Department License

Contact your health department to determine whether they will have any jurisdiction over your retail store. Some municipalities require any store offering food for resale to be inspected. Should they find faults in your facility, you will be required to have them corrected before they will issue a license.

Fire Department Permit

A permit from the fire department, also referred to as an occupational permit, will be required before opening. The fire department inspectors will be interested in checking extension cords, fire exits, extinguisher placements, the use of flammable materials and sprinkler systems before you open.

Based upon the size of the building, the local and national fire code and the number of exits, the fire inspectors will establish a "capacity number" of people permitted in the building at one time. Follow their guidelines strictly, even if this means turning away customers because you've reached capacity.

Building and Construction Permit

Should you plan to do any renovating to the store that is going to change the structural nature of the building, you may need a local building permit. Permit approval for retrofitting a building not previously used for cooking/baking may take time, so apply early.

Building permits are generally issued from the local Building and Zoning Board. You will need to contact the building inspector with your blueprints or plans to initially determine if a permit is required. Should a permit be required, he or she will inspect your plans to ensure that they meet all the local and federal ordinances and codes.

Once the plans are approved, a building permit will be issued. The building inspector will make periodic inspections of your work at various stages of completion to ensure that the actual construction is conforming to the approved plans.

Sign Permit

Many local city governments are beginning to institute sign ordinances and restrictions. These ordinances restrict the sign's size, type, location and lighting, and the proximity of the sign to the business. The owners or managers of a shopping mall or shopping center may also further restrict the use and placement of signs.

Federal Identification Number

All employers, partnerships and corporations must have a Federal Identification Number. This number will be used to identify the business on all tax forms and other licenses. To obtain a Federal Identification Number, fill out Form #554, obtainable from the IRS; use their Web registration at www.irs.gov, or enroll by phone by calling 800-829-4933.

Opening the Store's Bank Account

Opening a business bank account is a great deal more important than at first it may appear. If you received your financing through a local commercial bank, it would be suggested you also use this bank for your business account, if it fills all your needs.

Take plenty of time to shop around for the bank that will serve you the best. Many smaller banks are better suited for personalized service. When you go into a prospective bank, ask to see the bank manager. Tell him or her of your plans and what your needs are. Look at what each bank charges for check and deposit transactions and all other service charges.

As a retail store, it is important that you take credit and debit (ATM) cards. High-end stores may find they have customers interested in using Diner's Club and American Express. If you are in a tourist area attracting international travelers, ask your bank about accepting other types of charge cards. Compare credit card fees and card processing equipment fees. Even a small percentage can add up to a great deal of money over the years.

Insurance

Properly insuring a retail store is similar to the coverage of any business enterprise where members of the public are in frequent attendance. Liability protection is of the utmost concern. Product liability is also desirable, as the consumption of food and beverages always presents a hazard. (See Chapter 15 on food security issues.) At the very least, your business will need fire, liability and workers' compensation insurance. A discussion with your agent will help determine which insurance policies you should purchase. Your franchiser, lessor, mortgage holder or investors may also have specific insurance requirements that need to be taken into account.

Workers' Compensation Insurance

Workers' compensation insurance covers loss due to statutory liability as a result of an employee's on-the-job personal injury or death. Some states also provide for stress-related claims. This insurance coverage pays all medical treatment and costs plus a percentage of the employee's salary due to missed time resulting from the injury. Workers' compensation insurance is mandatory in most states. Failure to comply can result in large penalties and fines. Be certain to obtain all the information that pertains to your particular state.

Organizing Pre-Opening Activities

Opening a retail store or any business is a great test of anyone's organizational and managerial abilities. It is imperative that communication be maintained with your key personnel. Keep track of the assignments that need to be completed, who the assignments are delegated to and when they must be completed. Allow plenty of time for assignments and projects to be accomplished. Even the seemingly simplest task may uncover a web of tangles and delays. Delegate responsibilities whenever possible, but above all else, keep organized. Maintain a collective composure and deal with people and problems on a level and consistent basis and you'll be off to a great start.

Pre-Opening Promotion

Described below are some pre-opening promotional ideas. It should be noted that there is a distinction between promotion and advertising. Promotion involves creating an interest in a new project usually at little or no cost. (You'll find additional marketing and promotional information in Chapters 9 and 10.)

As soon as possible, put up the new store sign or a temporary sign briefly explaining the name of the new store, specialties, hours of operation and the opening date. By nature, people are curious about what is occurring in their neighborhood; give them something to start talking about. This is perhaps the best and least expensive promotion you can start: good buzz!

- Meet with the advertising representatives for the local papers. Determine advertising costs and look into getting a small news story published describing the store.

- Have plenty of business cards on hand as soon as possible. They're a great source of publicity.

- Join the Better Business Bureau and the local chamber of commerce. Besides lending credibility to your business, they often can supply you with some very good free publicity and an opportunity to network with peers.

- When you place your employment ad in the classified section, always list the type of retail store and location. This inexpensive classified advertising will help spread the word.

- Plan a grand opening celebration! That's an excellent reason for the local news to feature you. Create Grand Opening advertising such as a door hanger campaign or your first series of newspaper ads with a discount coupon.

Contacting Purveyors and Suppliers

As soon as you have funding for inventory, you need to establish a relationship with the manufacturers' distributor or rep group. This process can take four months or more, as the retail cycle dictates what is available for some items. You'll also need time to negotiate prices, establish lines of credit and "test" potential choices. (Chapter 11 continues the discussion on this topic.)

Approximately six to eight weeks before the scheduled opening date, it will be necessary to contact all the local suppliers (any company supplying products not for resale) and meet with their sales representatives. It would be advisable to have your store manager and other key personnel attend.

Opening Labor

Before the opening date, you may have a variety of people on the payroll. You could hire temporary help, but why not hire people who will be working in the store? By working together to create the store, you'll foster an invaluable team spirit. If needed, hire some temporary "muscle" to help with the heavy lifting, shelf assembly and other projects.

A time clock should certainly be used during this period for better control. Overtime must be carefully monitored and, if at all possible, avoided. This will require a great deal of organization between assignments and scheduling. (To learn more about hiring employees and payroll activities, see Chapters 7 and 16.)

Public Utilities

Notify public utility companies of your intention to be operating by a certain date. Allow plenty of lead-time for completion.

Phone Company

You will need at least two phone lines for any retail store. Don't forget about data lines if you need dial-up service for your Internet and a fax line. Don't lose customers because they can't get through. You should have two phones in the offices and one to two extensions at the register or order-taking area. Place local emergency numbers at all phones.

Gas and Electric Companies

Some major equipment will need special hookups that can only be completed by trained technicians of either the gas or electric company (or their authorized representatives) or licensed equipment installers (electricians, plumbers or factory support personnel). They should be contacted as early as possible to evaluate the amount of work required. In many cases, they will need to schedule the work several weeks ahead of time.

Water

If you will need water as a recipe ingredient or for beverages, you'll need to determine whether you need a filtering or softening system. Water is different in all parts of the country due to the type of chemical particles it contains. Water that has been subjected to a chemical treatment plant may contain a high level of chlorine. Chemical particles in the water can have a particularly bad effect in the brewing of fresh coffee. Water quality and mineral composition can affect foods using water. Several companies now market filtering devices that attach directly to the water lines. If prescribed, filters need only be connected to the water lines that are used for drinking/cooking water. Discuss your particular situation with your state's Department of Natural Resources and the sales representative for your coffee supplier.

Security Needs

Locksmith

A registered or certified locksmith can rekey the locks as soon as you occupy the building. Keys to locked areas should be issued on a "need-to-have" basis. The locksmith can set door locks so that certain keys may open some doors, but not others. Only the owner and manager should have a master key to open every door. Each key will have its own identification number and "Do Not Duplicate" stamped on it. Should there be a security breach, you can easily see who had access to that particular area. The store should be entirely rekeyed when key-holding personnel leave or someone looses his or her keys. Safe combinations should periodically be changed by the locksmith.

Fire and Intrusion Alarms

Every store should have a system for fire, smoke and heat detection and, depending upon your location, for intrusion and holdup. Check with your fire marshall for your store's fire detection and suppression requirements. They may also direct you towards a reputable fire and safety service company.

The fire-detection system consists of smoke monitors and heat sensors, strategically placed around the building. This system must be audible for evacuations and directly connected to either the fire department or a private company with 24-hour monitoring service. In newer buildings, the sensors also activate the sprinkler system.

Depending upon your community, the installation of an alarm system in the store is almost a necessity. The loss of business and profits due to burglary, vandalism or arson is not to be gambled upon. The installation of an alarm system will increase the value of the property, and a 24-hour monitored system may make you eligible with your insurance company for a rate reduction of 5 to 10 percent on the insurance premium.

Support Service Providers

Sanitation Service

A retail store of any size has a great deal of waste. In order to preserve a proper health environment, the services of a trash removal or sanitation service company will be required. (Waste and recycling issues are detailed in Chapter 14.)

If your local municipality or shopping center/mall owner does not provide trash removal, gather quotes from all the sanitation companies in the area. Prices may vary considerably depending upon who purchases the dumpsters. You may wish to get advice from your health department for the selection. Any service contract should contain provisions for the following:

- Dumpsters with locking tops.
- Periodic steam cleaning of the dumpsters.
- Fly pesticide sprayed on the inside of the dumpster.
- Number of days for pickup.
- Extra pickups for peak periods.

Parking Lot Maintenance

Many mall/shopping centers include parking maintenance in your lease. If it is not noted, negotiating this as sharing the cost with other merchants makes the most sense. If you are responsible for your own parking area, remember that parking lots will need periodic maintenance besides the daily duty of light sweeping and picking up of any trash. Painting new lines for the parking spaces should be done annually. Blacktop surfaces will also require a sealant to be spread over the surface periodically. This stops water from seeping into it. Winter climates will require snow removal and possibly salting and sanding of the lot. Most of these services may be purchased under contract.

Plumber

A local plumber will be needed to handle any miscellaneous work and emergencies that may come up. The plumber must have 24-hour emergency service.

Electrician

An electrician will be needed when equipment is moved or installed. If it has not been done already, the electrician should check out and label all the circuits and breakers in the building. The electrician should also be on 24-hour emergency service.

Refrigeration Service

If you offer foodstuffs that require refrigeration or freezing, you'll need a refrigeration company that can respond quickly to emergencies 24 hours a day. At any given time, the refrigeration systems and freezers could go out, which may result in the loss of several thousand dollars in inventory. Some services will offer monitoring and be able to respond should a refrigerated display or freezer malfunction during off hours.

Exterminator

Exterminators must be licensed professionals with excellent local references. Extermination methods should comply with local health department regulations and be guaranteed food-safe. Exterminators can eliminate any pest-control problems, such as rats, cockroaches, ants, termites, flies, etc. Have several companies come in to appraise the building. They are experts and can read the "tell-tale" signs that might otherwise be missed. The company selected should be signed to a service contract as soon as possible. This is not an area to cut corners or try to do it yourself—it won't pay in the long run.

Plant/Landscape Maintenance

A professional plant-care person and/or landscaper can provide all the necessary services to plant, rotate, water, transplant and arrange indoor and outdoor plant décor. Contact companies in the area to get their opinions, quotes and references. They must be made aware that they are working in an environment where toxic sprays may only be used with the approval of the health department, and, even then, very cautiously.

Heating, Ventilation and Air-Conditioning

You will need the services of a heating, ventilation and air-conditioning (HVAC) company that can respond 24 hours a day, at a moment's notice. Make certain the company is reliable with many references. Losing the heating system in the winter or the air-conditioning in the summer can damage temperature-sensitive merchandise and put undo strain on your staff and customers.

Janitorial Service

Depending upon the size and operating hours of the store, you may wish to use the services of a professional cleaning company with experience in retail establishments. Cleanliness has an important effect upon your image to customers and employee morale. The maintenance service company selected must have impeccable references. The company should be insured against liability and employee pilferage. Employees should be bonded. You will probably need to give the owner of the company his or her own keys to the entrance, maintenance closets, security system and possibly the office for cleaning.

Coffee Service Vendor

Major coffee distributors offer complete turnkey set-ups for serving your customers coffee. They will provide, at no charge, the equipment necessary for coffee service including: brewing machines, filters, vacuum pots, serving pots and maintenance and installation of all equipment. All that is required from you is to sign a contract stating you will buy their coffee exclusively. The price of all the equipment and maintenance is typically included in the price of the coffee.

Florist

Should you decide to have fresh-cut flowers, you will need to contact a local florist. Each week the florist will deliver cut flowers or plants of your choice.

7

Successful Employee Relations and Labor Cost Control

The most important investment you'll ever make for your business is in the people who work for and with you. No customer will return, no equipment will save time, no business will grow without employees. From the janitor to the store manager, every person plays an important role in your success. Even in the smallest store, you cannot do it alone. You'll need at least a part-timer or you'll quickly burn out. Having great employees starts with being a great boss.

The Value (and Cost) of Employees

Employees directly control service quality. It is a fact that a disgruntled employee will not produce or perform as well as a satisfied one. Yet, it is bewildering to note that many owners/managers fail to make the employee's job any easier or more enjoyable with modern training procedures.

"But it takes so long to train someone," you say. Training is an investment.

Without thorough training, the time you think you save will cost you dearly—in mistakes, lack of productivity, employee turnover and customer dissatisfaction.

You must make every conceivable effort to relieve employees of "busy" work and make their jobs more rewarding—the results can only be positive! Unfortunately, most business owners cannot substantiate or rationalize any investment in an employee's comfort or training because they feel the employee will probably quit in a month or two anyway. They think, "Why bother?" Of course, this starts the cycle all over again.

Employees are one of the greatest resources a business has, but this resource will be wasted if you do not first recognize it, and then supply the proper incentive and motivation necessary to harvest it.

Take the initiative to build a happy and productive staff, because you are the only one who can! Even simple accommodations, such as separate employee lockers, restrooms and break rooms, can make all the difference. Beyond physical accommodations and even pay raises, what employees need are satisfying work, being recognized for their contribution and understanding that life can be complex. Create a respectful environment where people feel comfortable to express their ideas, ask for help (in their business and personal life) and where every person has value. This doesn't mean you have to be pals with your employees; it simply means that you enjoy sharing your business success with them.

You must provide employees with:

- Fair and just wages
- Better training
- Insurance programs
- Flexible scheduling
- Shorter work weeks
- Childcare and transportation vouchers
- Incentive plans
- Proper tools to increase productivity, reduce stress and maximize safety
- Safe, clean working conditions
- Proper training and evaluations
- Financial security, if possible

- Adequate benefit packages
- An opportunity for advancement
- An amicable, structured and just working environment

The cost of providing these basic necessities, which have eluded many industries for so long, can be easily substantiated when compared to the cost of losing—and the cost of replacing—a discontented skilled employee. Your customers expect that the people who wait on them in your gourmet store are knowledgeable, service-oriented and have a passion for their job.

First, consider the indirect cost to the store when an unmotivated and unhappy employee provides poor service to a regular customer. Just as word-of-mouth can be great advertising, it can also cause the store to come crumbling to the ground from comments like, "The people in the store can never answer my questions" or "They have a great selection but the help is very rude."

Discontented employees will not be concerned about looking out for the store's interests. Why should employees care about the store's profits when they feel unappreciated or barely make enough to survive?

Consider the direct cost of replacing an employee: recruiting expense, interviewer's salary and time, administrative costs, training expense, medical exams, the loss of sales and the cost of materials due to training mistakes, the labor cost paid before the employee's full productivity is reached and the trainer's and supervisor's salaries. Consider the cost of termination: paperwork, exit interviewing and, possibly, unemployment compensation. According to the American Management Association, the cost to replace an employee who leaves is, conservatively, 30 percent of their annual salary. For those with skills in high demand, the cost can rise to a frightening 1.5 times their annual salary. Your ability to retain the kind of workers you want and need has a direct impact on the profitability and effectiveness of your organization.

The following sections will describe the hiring process, from the initial interview through the employee's termination.

Hiring Store Employees

The key to hiring good, competent employees is to put aside personal prejudices and select one applicant over another only because you feel he or she will have a better chance of being successful at the job. What a potential employee is qualified and capable of doing is often quite different from what he or she actually will do. The purpose of this section is to provide the interviewer with the information necessary to determine if the applicant has the qualities needed.

A Shortage of Service Labor

The fastest growing job sector is service. This can in many communities lead to a shortage of people suited for the job. Service jobs require cash-handling, organization and people skills. These skills, along with a strong work ethic, are critical to your success. However, you may find it difficult to fill these positions. The shortage of workers is not unique to the labor side of the equation; good management is also hard to find. In fact, as the members of the Baby Boom generation start retiring in 2011, the U.S. Department of Labor predicts the situation will worsen as these 76 million people exit the nation's labor pool.

You may find yourself in a position of "building" the ideal employee with on-the-job training and schooling. There are some advantages and disadvantages. It takes dedication to mentor and develop an employee; however, the reward for you and your business can be worth the time. Start by developing a list of skills that you'd like in the "ideal" employee, then look for ways to teach that: training classes in the local community college, etiquette classes and posture classes at a modeling school. Try Business Training Library (www.bizlibrary.com) to "borrow" training videos and seek the help of community college and high school counselors. They can also help you develop a mentoring program.

In addition, service businesses are extending their recruiting efforts beyond traditional methods, such as newspaper ads or signs posted in the store, to high school and college campus recruitment, retirement communities, state agencies and the Internet.

Key Points for Conducting Employment Interviews

- Treat all applicants considerately and show a genuine interest in them, even if they have little or no chance of obtaining the job.

- Make certain that you are on time and ready to receive the applicant. Arriving late or changing appointment dates at the last minute will give the applicant the impression that you are unorganized and that the store is run in the same manner.

- Know the job being offered thoroughly. You cannot possibly match someone's abilities with a job you do not know or understand completely.

- All interviews must be conducted in private, preferably in the interviewer's office. Interruptions must be kept to a minimum.

- Make the applicant feel at ease. Have comfortable chairs and possibly beverages available. Speak in a conversational, interested tone.

- Applicants will be full of questions about the job, its duties, the salary, etc. Newspaper advertisements tell only a little about the job and your company, so allow plenty of time for this important discussion.

- Whenever possible, let the applicants speak. You can learn a great deal about them by the way they talk about themselves, past jobs, former supervisors and school experiences. Watch for contradictions, excuses and, especially, the applicant being on the defensive or speaking in a negative manner. Avoiding subjects is an obvious indication that there was some sort of problem there in the past; be persistent about getting the whole story, but don't be overbearing. Come back to it later if necessary.

- Never reveal that you may disapprove of something an applicant has done or said; always appear open-minded. On the other hand, don't condone or approve of anything that is obviously in error.

- Always ask a few questions they don't expect and aren't prepared for: What do they do to relax? What are their hobbies? What is the last book they read? Try to understand their attitudes, personalities and energy levels.

- Perhaps one of the most useful things you can ask when interviewing prospective employees is: What were your favorite parts of your previous job? Look to see if the things they liked to do with previous employers fit with the things you'll be asking them to do for you. This is significant; it is important to cross-train employees to do as many jobs as possible, and it helps to know which of those jobs will be a good fit.

- Often in interviewing prospective service employees, you'll get two types of applicants: those who say they prefer the "people part" of the job (talking to customers, serving customers, running the cash register) and those who like the "store part" of the job.

- Be sure to ask at least one behavior-based question; this will be very useful in getting at how an applicant responds in real-life work situations and how well he or she is able to handle them.

Unlawful Pre-Employment Questions

This section is not intended to serve on behalf of or as a substitute for legal counsel, or even as an interpretation of the various federal and state laws regarding equal and fair employment practices. The purpose of this section is only to act as a guide to the type of questions that may and may not be legally asked of a potential employee. For more information on the topic, contact your State Labor Board.

A discussion of this subject with both the state and federal labor offices and your lawyer would be in order. Standard employment applications may be purchased at your local office supply store. Before you use these forms, let your lawyer examine one to make certain that it doesn't contain or insinuate any questions that might be considered illegal.

The Federal Civil Rights Act of 1964 and other state and federal laws ensure that a job applicant will be treated fairly and on an equal basis, regardless of race, color, religious creed, age, sex or national origin.

In order to support these regulations, you cannot ask certain questions of applicants concerning the aforementioned categories. There is a fine line between what may and may not be asked of applicants. Use basic common sense concerning the type of questions you ask. Any illegal question would have no bearing on the outcome of the interview anyway, so avoid questions that are related to, or might evoke an answer that infringes upon, the applicant's civil rights.

- Age is a sensitive pre-employment question, because the Age Discrimination in Employment Act (www.eeoc.gov/policy/adea.html) protects employees aged 40 years and older.
  - It is permissible to ask an applicant to state his or her age if it is fewer than 18 years to determine if they will require a state-issued work permit. The U.S. Department of Labor provides information on child labor laws at www.dol.gov/dol/topic /youthlabor/index.htm, as can your State Labor Board.

  - If you need the date of birth for internal reasons; for example, computations with respect to a pension or profit-sharing plan, this information can be obtained after the person is hired.

- It is permissible to ask an applicant if he or she uses drugs or smokes. The application also affords an employer the opportunity to obtain the applicant's agreement to be bound by the employer's drug and smoking policies. The application also affords an employer an opportunity to obtain the applicant's agreement to submit to drug testing.

- Whether an applicant has friends or relatives working for the employer may be improper if the employer gives a preference to such applicants.

- Credit rating or credit references have been ruled discriminatory against minorities and women.

- Whether an applicant owns a home has been held to be discriminatory against minority members, since a greater number of minority members do not own their own homes.

- While questions about military experience or training are permissible, questions concerning the type of discharge received by an applicant have been held to be improper, because a high proportion of other-than-honorable discharges are given to minorities.

- The Americans with Disabilities Act prohibits general inquiries about disabilities, health problems and medical conditions. The U.S. Department of Labor offers ADA information for employers at www.dol.gov/odep/pubs/adabro/employ.htm.

A list of prohibited questions, some of which are obvious but used to illustrate the point:

- How tall are you, anyway?
- What color are your eyes?
- Do you work out at the gym regularly?
- Do you or anyone you know have the HIV?
- Did you get any workers' comp from your last employer?
- How old are you, anyway?
- Have you been in prison?
- Are you really a man?
- Do you rent or own your home?
- Have you ever declared bankruptcy?
- What part of the world are your parents from?
- Are you a minority?
- Is English your first language?
- I can't tell if you're Japanese or Chinese. Which is it?
- So which church do you go to?
- Who will take care of the kids if you get this job?
- Is this your second marriage, then?

- Just curious: Are you gay?
- Are you in a committed relationship right now?
- How does boyfriend feel about you working here?

Screening Potential Employees

Screening job applicants will enable you to reject those candidates who are obviously unsuitable before you schedule a lengthy interview. This saves everyone time and money. The preliminary screening can be done by an assistant manager or someone knowledgeable about the store's employment needs and practices. Potential job candidates may then be referred to the manager for intensive interviews.

All applicants should leave feeling they have been treated fairly and had an equal opportunity to present their case for getting the job. As previously stated, this is an important part of public relations.

Base your preliminary screening on the following criteria:

- **Experience.** Is the applicant qualified to do the job? Examine past job experience. Check all references.

- **Appearance.** Is the applicant neatly dressed? Remember, he or she will be dealing with the public; the way the applicant is dressed now is probably better than the way he or she will come to work.

- **Personality.** Does the applicant have a personality that will complement the other employees' and impress customers? Is he or she outgoing, but not overbearing?

- **Legality.** Does the applicant meet the legal requirements?

- **Availability.** Can the applicant work the hours needed? commute easily?

- **Health and physical ability.** Is the applicant capable of doing the physical work required? All employees hired should be subject to approval only after a complete physical examination by a mutually approved doctor.

Make certain the application is signed and dated.

All applicants at this point should be divided into one of the three following categories:

- **Interview applicant.** If you are not the decision-maker in hiring, refer the applicant to the manager and/or supervisor to schedule an interview. Involve others who will be responsible for the new hire. You'll show your management team that their opinions are important and you'll improve your hiring practices.

- **Reject.** Describe the reasons for rejection and place the application on file for future reference. Never make written comments that are in any way derogatory as previously described in the discrimination areas. Check with your lawyer on recommended retention times for these applications.

- **Prospective file.** Any applicant who is not qualified for this position but may be considered for other areas of the store should be placed in a prospective applicant file.

Once you have categorized all prospective candidates, be courteous and let those in categories #2 and #3 know that they have not been selected for the position. For those in the "future prospect" category, ask permission to contact them when another opening arises.

What to Look for in Potential Store Employees

- **Stability.** You don't want employees to leave in two months. Look at past employment dates. Stability also refers to the applicant's emotional makeup.

- **Leadership qualities.** Employees must be those who are achievers and doers, not individuals who have to be led around by the hand. Look at past employment positions and growth rate.

- **Motivation.** Why is the applicant applying to this store? Why the retail industry in general? Is the decision career-related, or temporary? Does the applicant appear to receive his or her motivation from within, or by a domineering other, such as a spouse or parent?

- **Independence.** Is the applicant on his own? Does he or she appear to be financially secure? At what age did he or she leave home? For what reasons? (Be careful about asking personal questions, as they can easily be misconstrued as improper.)

- **Maturity.** Is the individual mentally mature enough to work in a busy and demanding environment? Will he or she be able to relate and communicate with other employees and customers who may be much older (or younger)?

- **Determination.** Does the applicant seem to always finish what he or she starts? Does he or she seem to look for, or retreat from, challenges? Examine time at school and at their last job.

- **Work habits.** Is the applicant aware of the physical work involved in the position? Has the applicant done similar work? Does the applicant appear neat and organized? Look over the application; is it filled out per the instructions? neatly? in ink? Examine past jobs for number and rate of promotions and raises.

The Final Selection and Decision

Deciding to whom you'll offer the job is often a difficult choice. You may have more than one qualified applicant, so who do you select?

Always base your choice on the total picture the applicants have painted of themselves through the interviews, resumes and applications. Gather advice from those who interviewed or had contact with the individuals. Not only will this help you reach the correct decision, but will also make the rest of your staff feel a part of the management decision-making team. Whomever you select, he or she must be someone you feel good about having around, someone you will enjoy working with and whom you feel will have a very good chance of being successful at the job.

When you offer the job, make certain the applicant fully understands the following items before accepting the position:

- **Salary.** Starting pay, salary range, expected growth rate, the day payroll is issued, company benefits, vacations, insurance, etc.
- **Job description.** List of job duties, hours, expectations, etc.
- **Report date.** Time and date of first day of work and to whom he or she should report.
- **Job attire.** You probably talked about this during the interview, but make certain they understand your rules about facial hair, dangling bracelets and other appearance issues before they start. Emphasize how they relate to good customer service and employee safety.
- **Drug testing.** If you require drug testing, clarify that the procedures and their employment would not begin before the testing is completed with negative results. For information on employment drug testing, visit the U.S. Chamber of Commerce's Web site at www.uschamber.com.

Rejecting Applicants

Rejecting applicants is always an unpleasant and difficult task. Many applications will be rejected almost immediately. Some applicants will ask the reason for rejection. Always be honest, but use tact in explaining the reasoning behind the decision. Avoid a confrontation, explaining only what is necessary to settle the applicant's questions. Usually it will be sufficient to say, "We accepted an applicant who was more experienced" or "…who is better qualified."

As mentioned before, some applications may be transferred into a "prospective file" for later reference. Inform the applicant of this action, but don't give the impression that he or she has a good chance of being hired, nor state a specific date when you will be looking for new employees.

Employee Handbook/Personnel Policy Manual

Federal law mandates that all employers, regardless of size, have written policy guidelines. Employee handbooks/policy manuals are used to familiarize new employees with company policies and procedures. They also serve as guides to management personnel.

Creating a formal written policy could keep you out of court, prevent problems and misunderstandings, save time spent answering common questions and look more professional to your employees. Explaining and documenting company policy to your employees has been proven to increase productivity, compliance and retention. However, what you say and don't say in your written policy can also put your business at risk. The Online Women's Business Center operated by the SBA explains various issues relating to employee handbooks at www.onlinewbc.gov/docs/manage/hrpol_idx.html.

Lack of communication, along with inadequate policies and guidelines, have been cited as major factors in workplace legal disputes. Failure to inform or notify employees of standard policies has resulted in the loss of millions of dollars in legal judgments. Simply not being aware that their actions violated company policy has been an effective defense for many terminated employees. Most important is to have the employee sign a document stating he or she has received, reviewed, understands and intends to comply with all policies in the manual.

Writing Your Employee Policy Manual

If you have ever written a policy document before, you know how time-consuming it can be. Even if you were a lawyer, it would likely take you 40 hours to research and write a comprehensive employee manual. To pay someone to draw one up for you can cost thousands of dollars. There are a variety of human resource Web sites that can assist you with writing a custom employee manual, or you can purchase standardized forms (see Human Resource Supply at www.humanresourcesupply.com/emhanpolman1.html, or Template Zone's Office Policy Manual 2004 at www.templatezone.com /employee-handbook/office-policy-manual.asp). Your attorney can also guide you through this process and can read your final version for compliance with state and federal laws.

Personnel File

Once the applicant is hired, an individual personnel file should be set up immediately. It should contain the following information:

- Application
- Form W-4 and Social Security number
- Name, address and phone number
- Emergency contact information and phone number
- Employment date
- Job title and pay rate
- Past performance evaluations
- Signed form indicating receipt and acceptance of Employee Handbook
- Termination date, if applicable, and a detailed account of the reasons for termination

Employees may also elect to have medical alert information (such as allergies) in their files for emergency situations.

Training

The most serious problem facing the retail industry today is the lack of trained personnel and structured, industry-wide training programs. This means that you may hire an "experienced" employee, only to discover they lack the skills you anticipated or simply don't meet your customer service standards. New employees are often thrown into jobs, with little or no formal training. While on the job they must gather whatever information and skills—whether correct or not—they can. Managers regard training as a problem that must be dealt with—quickly and all at once—so that the new trainee can be brought up to full productivity as soon as possible. As a business owner, you can stop that cycle by thoroughly training and cross-training your staff.

Getting employees to do things right means taking the time to train them properly from the start so that they understand what needs to be done, how to do it and why it should be done that way. Effective training, however, involves more than simply providing information. Training is not a problem, and it cannot be "solved" and then forgotten. Managers and supervisors at every level must soon realize that training is a continual process, as is learning; it must never stop.

The most effective training technique is interactivity. Get people to stand up and do things. Show them how to arrange the display, roll-play how to handle difficult customers, teach them proper hand-washing procedures, demonstrate how a kitchen tool is used and teach them how to operate equipment.

However, training is also more than teaching skills, such as running the cash register. Employees must know not only their job and how to perform it, but how their performance affects others in their jobs in other parts of the store. They must visualize their position as an integral part of an efficient machine, not as a separate, meaningless function.

Telling an employee that his or her position and performance is crucial to the store's success and showing the reasons why are two entirely different things. Reinforce your expectations by demonstrating the proper methods, as well as explaining the ramifications of varying from these procedures.

Apply this principle of demonstrating rather than lecturing to illustrate your points with all of your employees, and you will have the basis for a good training program and good employee relations.

Orientation and Instruction

Your "new hire" orientation is the first step in thorough training. The entire orientation will take less than thirty minutes; unfortunately, however, it is rarely done. There is no excuse for not giving the new employee a proper introduction before he or she starts the actual training.

Described below are some basic orientation practices:

- Introduce the new employee to yourself and the company.
- Introduce the new employee to all of the other employees.
- Introduce the new employee to the trainer and supervisor.
- Explain the company's employee and personnel policies. Present him or her with a copy and have them return the next day to sign the "I have received and read" commitment.

Outline the objectives and goals of the training program.

- Describe the training and where and how it will take place.
- Describe the information that will be learned.
- Describe the skills and attitudes that will be developed.

Set up a schedule for the employee. It should include:

- The date, day and time to report to work during training.
- Who will be doing the training and who the supervisor is.
- What should be learned and accomplished each day.
- The date when the training should be completed.

Ideally, the employee's regular supervisor does all of the training. The trainer must be a model employee who is thoroughly knowledgeable about and experienced in the job. He or she must be able to communicate clearly and have a great deal of patience and understanding.

The trainee must be taught the how, why, when and where of the job. This is best accomplished by following the trainer's example and methods. After confidence is built, the employee may attempt to repeat the procedure under the watchful eye of the trainer.

Once the employee has completed the training, the trainer or supervisor should prepare a final written report and evaluation. This report should describe the strengths and weaknesses of the trainee, their knowledge of the job, quality of work, attitude and a general appraisal of the employee. After the manager reviews this report, all three parties should meet to discuss the training period. The employee should be congratulated on successfully completing the training program.

A review of the final report would be in order and then filed in the employee's personnel file for future reference. Ask the employee's opinion on the training program; he or she may have some thoughts on improving it. This same question should be presented to the employee after two weeks of work. Find out if the training program adequately prepared the trainee for the actual job.

Outside Help in Training

When training sessions involve several people or even the entire staff, you might find it helpful to bring in outside support for your meetings. Look for business associates and experts in their fields who are interested in sharing their wisdom. Often just a phone call is enough inducement. Reward these people for their time and effort with a complimentary gift certificate.

There are other great resources for outside-training information available to assist in your training programs: videos, posters, books, software, etc. One great source for all these products is Atlantic Publishing (www.atlantic-pub .com, 800-541-1336).

Below are some ideas for speakers and topics to enhance your staff's knowledge.

- **Resale merchandise vendor**—Product features and benefits along with sales techniques and marketing ideas.
- **Health Department Inspector**—Health and sanitation practices/ requirements.
- **Equipment manufacturer representative**—Proper use of

equipment, maintenance and cleaning tips.

- **Community Service Police Officer**—Crime-prevention and response tips.
- **Fire Department Instructor**—Fire-prevention and emergency-response tips.
- **Bank Trainer**—Proper cash-handling techniques, counterfeit bill recognition.
- **Ergonomic Advisor**—Assess and review how people interact with machinery and facility. Teach people how to properly align body to minimize physical stress and fatigue.
- **Red Cross Instructor**—Basic first aid, the Heimlich Maneuver to stop choking and C.P.R. procedures.

Evaluating Performance

Evaluating each employee's job performance is a crucial element in developing a productive work environment and sound employee relations. Every employee must be aware of his or her strengths and which areas of his or her job performance need improvement.

Quarterly or periodic one-on-one evaluations help break down the communication barriers between management and employees. Many of an employee's work-related problems, thoughts and ideas can be revealed in the evaluation session. However, remember to keep in mind that evaluations are only a part of the communication process, and should not be considered a substitute for daily communication. You and your supervisory team must always be available to listen. Communication is an ongoing and continual process. Consider these points before filling out the evaluation forms:

- Know the employee's job description thoroughly. You are evaluating how well the employee meets the job requirements; you are not comparing against other employees nor evaluating the employee according to what you see as his or her potential.

- Always conduct the evaluation in private with no interruptions. Schedule each evaluation far enough apart so that there is plenty of time to discuss everything in one sitting.

- Don't let just one incident or trait—positive or negative—dominate the evaluation. Look at the whole picture over the entire time since the last evaluation.

- Evaluations should balance positive and negative attributes; never be one-sided. A primarily negative evaluation will almost never motivate a poor employee. Bring out some of his or her positive contributions and describe in detail what changes are needed. A completely negative evaluation will only scare the employee. Should a very negative evaluation be warranted, it is probable that the employee should have been terminated long ago.

- Review past evaluations, but don't dwell on them. Look for areas where improvement or a decline in performance has taken place.

- Always back up your thoughts and appraisals with specific examples.

- Allow plenty of time for the employee's comments. Remember, you could be wrong.

- If examples or circumstances that were never mentioned before come out in the evaluation, you are guilty of allowing the communication process to deteriorate.

- Don't cover too much material or expect the employee to make a drastic change overnight. An evaluation is only part in a series of continuous steps to direct the employee.

- Begin the evaluation with the employee's positive points and then direct the discussion to areas that need improvement.

- Certain personality traits and deficiencies may not always be changeable. Don't overemphasize them, but show how they might affect the employee's job performance and the performance of others.

- Finish the evaluation on a positive note. The employee should leave with a good feeling about his or her positive contributions to the store and know precisely what and how to improve on weaknesses.

- After the evaluation, make certain that you follow up on the thoughts, ideas and recommendations that were brought out during the evaluation. Without a follow-up, the evaluation is of little value.

- Evaluations are confidential. File them in the employee's personnel file only if no one else has access to them there.

Scheduling

The overall objective in scheduling is to place the most efficient employee at the job and shift where he or she will achieve maximum productivity at minimum expense. The greatest tool management has in controlling labor cost is scheduling, and yet scheduling is most often so poorly done that it becomes more a part of the problem than of the solution. In many cases, the employee's schedule is scribbled on a piece of paper or, worse, verbally communicated with little thought as to what is actually needed.

Properly preparing the weekly schedule for a store of fifteen employees may take between 60 to 90 minutes to complete. The individual preparing the schedule has to take into account many different factors such as:

- Peak periods (specific hours or days of the week).

- At what time maximum production must be reached.

- Special events that need additional assistance or require staff to leave the premises.

- The skill and productivity of each employee.

- Each employee's desired schedule: days off, hours, etc.

Only after several months of operation will you be able to accurately assess your precise labor needs. During the first couple of months, be sure you have plenty of employees available should it become suddenly busy. Many customers will understand that you have just opened and don't have all the bugs quite worked out yet, but they are still paying full price for everything. Don't get caught short on trained personnel. Your service on opening day should be consistent with that several months later. Use your best employees during peak hours, then schedule the other employees in sequence at the time you need them most.

Full-time employees should be cross-trained to perform two or more jobs so absences are less burdensome to the remaining staff and, most importantly, to your customers. There are many beneficial results from this situation. Scheduling will become a lot easier, as you have some employees willing to be shifted around to meet your needs. Employees who call in sick or leave without notice won't be as disruptive if you have people capable of handling their duties.

Many employees will enjoy performing multiple responsibilities, as they will not become as easily bored and will tend to feel like an integral part of the store. An employee who is involved, interested and concerned about the store will always be a better performer than one who is detached. The only possible disadvantage to this cross-training arrangement is that, when the employee does leave, he or she will be harder and more expensive to replace. Most likely, this thinking is shortsighted and contributes to higher employee turnover. If you never give employees the opportunity to develop and prove themselves because you are afraid they'll only leave in a few months, undoubtedly they will. Every employee should be given the opportunity for growth.

Should over-scheduling occur, employees can be assigned tasks that will produce future labor savings or bring in more customers, such as mailing newsletters or cleaning and organizing work areas. Additional unneeded employees can be sent home. Check with your Labor Board regarding these regulations. Under most state rulings, the employee who is scheduled to work and then is not needed must be compensated in some manner; usually paid a minimum of three hours' wages.

The store's sales history is another important tool in scheduling for productivity. Don't forget special events. For example, holidays and tourist events are as important to anticipate as business downturns.

In recent years, computer software has helped management enormously in scheduling employees. This software simplifies the time-consuming, labor-intensive manual processes involved in scheduling employees, maximizing resources, controlling labor costs and retaining a qualified staff. Most software systems enable the manager to quickly determine the right employee for each position and shift. Most of the software is easily integrated with time, attendance and payroll systems. All of these systems will save money and enhance employee satisfaction and retention. The software will range in price from a few hundred dollars to several thousand dollars. (You'll find more information on scheduling software in Chapter 12.) One good scheduling system with the option of an employee time clock is available from Atlantic Publishing (www.atlantic-pub.com, 800-541-1336).

Terminating an Employee

There comes a time when an unsatisfactorily performing employee, after being evaluated and given a fair opportunity to correct his or her deficiencies, must be terminated. Discharging an employee is always a difficult and unpleasant task, but it must be done for the good of the store. Although it may be an unpleasant experience, it is far worse to let the employee stay on. Before long, the entire staff's morale will drop, causing a decrease in productivity.

Deciding whether an employee should be terminated or retrained is difficult and often prejudiced by your inability to examine the entire picture of the employee's performance. The final decision to discharge an employee should be reached after carefully weighing the pros and cons—never in anger, when tired or under stress. Ask the employee's supervisor for an evaluation of the situation and the employee. Examine the employee's training, supervision and past evaluations. Make certain the employee has been given a fair opportunity to improve. Also, be certain that neither you nor any member of your management staff has in any way contributed to, caused or perpetuated the problem.

Letting Them Go

Immediately after reaching your decision to terminate, set up a meeting with the employee Don't let more than twenty-four hours go by; you don't want this information to leak out.

- Should the employee disagree with your reasoning or points, give him or her the opportunity to discuss them, but make sure you back up everything you say with proven facts and statements.
- Remain seated and calm during the proceedings; don't get up quickly or move suddenly.
- Never touch the employee, except when shaking hands. These actions may be misinterpreted and lead to a confrontation.
- Fill out a report on the termination proceedings, and file it in the employee's personnel file. This report will be important should the employee decide to challenge the action.
- Develop a plan to fill the vacancy as soon as possible. Keep in mind that it will take several months before a new employee can be brought up to full productivity and that, after training, he or she may not work out at all.

Although nothing can fully prevent a former employee from filing a lawsuit, there are ways to decrease the likelihood of litigation: Be honest with the employee about his or her performance and the reason for the termination, treat employees consistently and aggressively investigate claims of discrimination.

Above all, document the chances you've given employees to improve prior to your decision to terminate them. If a termination is challenged, and there are no records of the problems cited as reasons for termination and indicating opportunities given to correct these problems, there could be a problem. Keep in mind your notes don't have to be very detailed, but a dated description of a problem or of the employee's progress that is slipped into a personnel file helps dramatically.

Your other employees may perceive the termination of an employee as a threat to their security. You may even be looked upon as unfair or exceedingly harsh. Sometimes an explanation is needed to soothe the other employees. Never share derogatory thoughts, discriminatory comments or confidential information to your other employees. In most cases, though, the reasons will be obvious to them and they will be on your side.

Still, and again, document everything.

Exit Interviews

An exit interview is a valuable tool for the employer and the employee. You may learn things that you were previously unaware of and can correct with future employees, and they may learn how to become better employees in the future. Exit interviews can be conducted whenever an employee leaves; however, these are voluntary. You may find that terminated employees aren't particularly interested in talking any longer, so don't push the issue.

- The employee's supervisor should be present during the exit interview. He or she will be able to add support and witness the action. This is important, as the employee may use some legal means to gain a settlement.

- Conduct the exit interview in a private room with no interruptions.

Managing Your Team

It is imperative that you know how to manage and treat your employees. Make them a part of the team. Keep them informed of changes and get their feedback regarding changes. Employees oftentimes have excellent ideas that can lead to new market areas, innovations to existing products or services or new product lines or services that can improve your overall competitiveness. Remember, the best person to advise you on streamlining a job is the person who has to do it every day. Listen and learn.

8

Your Customers

Without customers, you don't have a store; you have a warehouse. Even purchasing an established store isn't an automatic guarantee of success. You'll need to keep current customers happy (some people hate change) and work to find new customers interested in your offerings.

Who Are Your Customers?

In researching and writing your business plan, you'll have learned tidbits about who your potential customers are. Now is be a good time to create an "ideal" customer. Understanding this person will help you stock the products they want, at the highest price they will pay, at the service level they expect.

As a new business, you will probably start with some assumptions that you'll need to assess and fine-tune after your doors are open.

Think about the type of people who are coming in.

- Look at how they are dressed: upscale singles in a rush, or mothers with kids in tow?

- Do they want purchasing guidance, or do they prefer to shop uninterrupted?

- How long do they take to make up their mind?

Why are they coming in?

- Buying for daily needs, or a special occasion?

- Are they searching for something specific, or browsing?

Where are they coming from or going to?

- Are they on their way home from work? after church? after a movie?

- How do they arrive (walk, drive, bus)? Is special packaging needed?

How did they find you?

- Are they coming to you through a phone directory listing?

- Do they bring in your newspaper coupons?

If you don't know much about your customers, ask! Introduce yourself and ask questions like:

- Is this your first time in?
- Do you live nearby?
- Did you find everything you wanted?
- Can we put you on our mailing list?
- Will you come back?

People, People, People

Even in the age of discount warehouses and e-commerce, face-to-face, one-on-one personalized service is your key to success. People want to be treated like individuals, and they will repeatedly do business with a store that does so. Connecting with your customers requires that you connect with them one-on-one.

So how do you connect? By being "in the present" with your customers. We have wrongly accepted the idea that doing many things at once, "multi-tasking," is effective. If you're taking a phone order and ringing up a sale, how much real attention will any of those tasks get? Do you think the potential customer on the phone or the customer at the counter will feel well-treated?

The truth is that we can really only focus on one thing at a time. When you talk to your staff or your customers, really talk to them and always listen more than you talk. Drop distractions, handle each item individually and then move on to the next. Presence is simply a lack of distraction. If you act distracted with your staff, they will keep asking the same questions or coming to you with the same problems. If you are distracted around your customers, they won't come back at all. Pay attention. People will notice and you will too.

Getting to Know Your Customers

In a business that lives and dies on personal connection, getting to know your customers is crucial. Go beyond the procedures of service, and start thinking of your customers as individuals. Numbers are important, but your relationship to your customers drives your business. Furthermore, the two easiest things to learn about your customers are also the most useful: who they are and what they like.

People love it when you remember who they are. It instantly makes them feel like they're insiders and makes them feel important in the eyes of their friends. Remember Norm on "Cheers"? Norm felt pretty comfortable and he definitely came back. As a manager, you probably know your regulars by name, but do you have a system in place that teaches your new staff who these important folks are? If you were a regular customer at a store and a counter person you had never seen came up and greeted you by name, wouldn't you feel like a celebrity?

You can train your employees to ask people's names and take time to remember faces. Have your customer service staff wear nametags—this is a great way to establish a rapport. Continually remind your staff that they are serving people, not anonymous shoppers. Using your customers' names makes it easier to remember them.

When you accept a personal check, a credit card or ask for a callback name, you have immediate access to their name. You can introduce yourself, "I'm Susan. If you need anything, please feel free to call and ask." If they give their names, repeat it to reinforce the memory. "Mrs. Jones, it was a pleasure to help you." Even if you don't know a customer's name, address them by looking them in the face, smiling and thanking them for coming in. If you are sincere, you'll have connected!

Now that you are talking to customers as individuals, the next step is to find out what they want as individuals. How? You must ask, but you also must remember not only what you've been told, but also what you've observed. If you are doing a good job serving customers, you'll soon have regulars.

Appreciation

What do you do to let your customers know that you appreciate them? If you recognize them and make them feel important, it will draw them closer to your store and further differentiate you in their eyes from your competitors. There are many ways to publicly recognize your customers. Below are a few ideas to get you thinking of ways to show your appreciation. Many can be done at little or no cost. However, unless you've actually taken time to get to know them, you won't be able to make your appreciation personal.

- Sponsor events where customers can be included in newspaper features.
- Hold a contest and include names and pictures in advertising.
- Send out thank-you notes along with special orders.

Bringing in New Customers

Your advertising and public relations efforts, along with building great word-of-mouth, is how you'll bring new customers to your store. (In Chapters 9 and 10, you'll find marketing and public relations ideas and resources.) One of the best ways to bring in new customers is to get your current customers talking. Word-of-mouth advertising is invaluable. Someone they trust—a friend, neighbor, co-worker or family member—relays the information. We will discuss word-of-mouth advertising later in this chapter.

Keeping your customers happy is a great way to create a positive "buzz" about your products and service. The remainder will talk about good communications and delighting customers. Do that and you'll have all the "buzz" you need!

How to Keep Customers Coming Back

Growing your business requires an ongoing effort to bring new customers to your door. It can take a significant investment—in time and money—to keep your name in front of potential customers. No matter how many new customers you bring in every day, it's how you keep them coming back that will make you profitable.

Investing your resources in building long-term customers is significantly less expensive (and more practical) than advertising for new customers. Even the largest city has a finite number of potential customers for your business, so once they grace your doors, you've got to keep them coming back.

You cannot succeed as a stand-alone retail store without excellent service. Variations of your entire product line are readily available at the nearest supermarket. Although the imported olives and hand-carved wooden spoons are superior to those mass-produced goods, it's your customer service that will keep people driving by the competitors to shop at your store.

Are you creating an environment that leaves customers feeling served and eager to come back? Are you holding staff meetings that leave your crew energized, or deflated? Are you, your management and your staff working independently, or as a complete whole towards a common goal?

Communicating with Your Customers

We all know first impressions last. If your customers have to battle for a parking space or drop by after a hard day's work, your first impression is that much more important. It's an opportunity to let them know they're welcome and you are there to help them tap into the joy of buying, preparing and eating fine foods and beverages.

Obviously, how you relate to your customers affects their opinion of you. That opinion then translates into potential loyalty, and loyalty boosts your bottom line. In fact, a 5 percent improvement in customer retention can translate into a 15–50 percent boost in profits. Those are serious numbers. In common terms, that simply means getting your regular customers to return one more time per month. Furthermore, it costs about five times as much to attract a new customer as it does to retain an existing one. Three things to focus on for retaining customers:

- Pay attention to your most profitable clients. Listen. Keep in touch. Find out what they want and need and why they've chosen you.
- If they go to your competition, find out why.
- If people are leaving empty-handed, ask why?

So how do you gather this information? In an establishment where people come and go quickly, this can be a challenge. Below are a few ideas to help you learn more:

- Tuck a prepaid postcard survey into every package. Ask your customers to rate your store, your products and your staff with questions like "Would you visit us again?" If you get a "no," take immediate action to determine why, and then fix the situation.
- Provide a comment section on your Web site.

- Create comment cards where customers rate your store. Have your staff hand these out to people over the counter. Offer discounts or promotional items for the return of the cards.

- Make a follow-up call to class attendees.

- Create a customer database to develop a line of communication through newsletters, remembrance programs and promotional mailings.

When communicating with your customers:

- Thank your customers for their business.

- Whenever you can, individualize your communications.

- Make it easy for them to communicate with you. If it is only one way, it isn't truly communication. If their opinions are important to you, they'll come back.
  - Include your phone number and Web address on all packaging, promotional materials and brochures.

- Listen to and act on customer suggestions.

- Inform customers of new or improved services. Put your PR wheels in motion.

- Tell customers of potential inconveniences like renovations, and stress their future benefits.

- Answer every inquiry, including complaints.

- Accommodate all reasonable requests for special orders.

- Empower employees to solve problems.

- Talk to your customers and employees so you can let them know you're listening and find out what's going on.

Customers for Life

Take care of your customers and your sales will take care of themselves. "Customers for life" means that once customers come to your store, they'll never be satisfied with your competitors. Simple, right? It also means that the real work of building sales doesn't happen with your advertising schedule or marketing plan, but face to face with your customers.

The key to building retail sales is to increase volume from your existing customer base. Think about it: If your customers were to return just one more time per month, that would be an increase in sales volume of between 15 and 50 percent! These are people who already know about you, live within an acceptable travel distance and will recommend you to their friends if you make them happy.

So how do you do this? Work on building loyalty, not just your per-sale average. Focusing only on the bottom line by pushing the most expensive item for their needs puts your customers second at best. If everyone who ever shopped at your store were so pleased that they couldn't wait to come back, what would your sales be like? If buying from you isn't a pleasant (and perhaps even a joyful) experience, what difference does it make how big the sale is since they won't be coming back?

This isn't to say that suggestive selling can't work. If it's done well, it can be very effective. However, it can backfire if it appears the goal is to just sell more, more, more. Your goal is to delight them, win their loyalty and put them first, first, first! If you were a store customer, what would bring you back again? Your service person being pushy and focusing on getting you to spend more money, or treating you like royalty?

Incentives

Incentives work because people do what they are rewarded for doing. It is as simple as that. Reward customers for coming back and they will. There are three basic ways to do this: discounts, promotions and customer loyalty programs.

Discounts

An effective discount actually gives your customers a deal and generates more profit for you. How? By making a sale you wouldn't have made otherwise. Discounting specific items can be profitable. For example, if a customer purchases a discounted item that has a 40 percent profit margin after the discount, instead of a similar item with 30 percent profit margin, your discount paid off! The customer is getting a deal and you're making more money.

Weekly sales are supposed to bring in new and returning customers. Once they are there, you have an opportunity to:

- **Cross-market impulse items.** Add eye-catching displays filled with appealing items next to sales merchandise.
- **Promote full-price accessories.** The mixer may be on sale, but the "must-have" attachment isn't.
- **Introduce companion products.** Display a specialty cookbook next to the pressure cookers that are on sale.
- **Free with purchase.** Some brand-name manufacturers prohibit product discounts; however, you can give them a free pound of gourmet coffee or a whisk with purchase.

Internal coupons can be a great way to increase repeat business. Three of the most widely used are:

- **Courtesy coupons.** These are wallet-sized coupons that your staff carries. They can be issued to customers and used on return visits. They are great if a customer has a complaint or has been inconvenienced somehow; they can be used to reward customers for their ongoing patronage.
- **Cross-marketing coupons.** If you sell them a coffee pot and grinder, hand out a discount coupon on their next three whole coffee bean purchases.

- **Companion coupons.** Encourage your regulars to bring a friend. You can offer a two-for-one special to be "shared" with a friend.

Promotions

Five great promotional opportunities are: birthdays, anniversaries, holidays , special events and festivals.

- **Birthdays and anniversaries.** Do you have an irresistible offer for patrons who are making birthday or anniversary purchases? You can get the dates of their special occasions when they sign up for your frequent-buyer program. (Hint: Let them know when they sign up that you're asking about these dates in order to offer them specials on their birthdays and anniversaries; otherwise they could feel their privacy is being invaded.) With this information, you can invite them to celebrate with a great wine or gourmet treat from your store. Also, make sure your offer is valid for more than just the actual date being celebrated—within the month is effective—because people need some flexibility in planning their special events.

- **Holidays.** The beauty of the holidays is that someone else advertises them. You don't have to tell your customers the winter holidays are coming, but you could put a flyer in with their October purchases about purchasing a deep-fat turkey fryer or imported holiday party favors.

- **Special events.** Special events can be a great way to promote business and goodwill. Have you thought of hosting a tea tasting, an all-chocolate celebration or participating in a community festival or charity fundraiser?

Special events can be held after-hours, where attendees can freely mingle throughout the store. Theme events are a great way to bring people in that might never have stepped through your door. These events can be held merely for the fun of it, or you can use the occasion to recognize employees or community leaders, or as fundraisers.

Product festivals are great reasons to invite customers to come back, and they're great things for customers to talk about. They highlight specific cuisines or products, and can be a great way to stir things up for staff and customers alike. You can run a festival on a specific night or for a specific time period—usually a week or two. Make sure, however, that the festival you hold is right for your establishment, and that it is run frequently enough to break up your routine, but infrequently enough to remain special. Do a memorable job and build a strong foundation for future events.

Product festivals usually coincide with seasonal items—raspberries, pumpkins, etc.—when the items are abundant and cheaper. Off-season festivals can be great for word-of-mouth—if you can find the product. People would love a fresh strawberry festival in January. Regional food items like King Cakes for Mardi Gras and blue corn tortillas might be just the ticket to attract new customers.

Community celebrations, festivals, farmers' markets and fairs can be a good venue for you to introduce your products to others beyond your neighborhood. Thoroughly research these venues before committing your staff to these labor-intensive events; you must comply with all state and local food service and health regulations. Your goal is to get people to sample your food goods, and come into your store for more!

A charity fundraiser can be a way to gain exposure for your store that pays off for everyone. It will improve your image and distinguish you from competitors. It doesn't have to be a break-even venture either, because you only give a portion of the proceeds to the cause. Ask your vendors and suppliers to donate items or share the hosting duties in exchange for promoting their wares and community goodwill. Enlist neighboring businesses to lower your costs and increase the donations. By working with complementary businesses, you also increase your chances of getting some in-depth news coverage of your event. The charity will also promote you to its supporters, which can bring new people through your door who want to support your business. (For more information on charity and PR, see Chapter 10.)

Frequent-Buyer Programs

Many businesses have found frequent-buyer programs are an excellent way to build loyalty and repeat business. Your frequent-buyer program should be simple for you and your customers. If you can get people to sign up for your program, you'll have a way to keep in touch. Ask for basic contact information (including e-mail if you wish to e-mail specials or a newsletter) and special events (birthdays, anniversaries) that warrant a special remembrance or discount.

Rewarding your customers for continued loyalty gives them an added incentive to choose you over the competition, and will help bring them back that extra time each month. Frequent-buyer programs usually come in variations on three basic forms:

- **Punch cards.** An inexpensive card that is typically issued for free and is punched every time the guest purchases a product. When they have purchased a certain number of items, they receive something free. The biggest plus of punch cards is they are easy to produce. The biggest negative is the ease with which they can be altered. Keeping the customers' cards, or duplicate cards, on the premises can help counter this.

- **Point systems.** These are often dollar-for-point systems in which a customer accrues points towards free merchandise. A point system is more complicated to implement than a punch card system.

- **Percentage-of-purchase programs.** This is the closest type to the airline programs, with customers paying full price for items while accruing dollar credits for future purchases. This gets people in the habit of thinking of their purchases as having a larger-than-normal value and keeps them coming to you.

Punch cards, point systems and percentage-of-purchase programs are all ways to monitor your customers' purchasing, reward them for coming back and increase your opportunities to delight them with your products and service. Take some time to figure out which is right for you.

Delighting Your Customers

Satisfaction isn't even close to good enough. It's an improvement on dissatisfaction, of course, but in today's market, it won't keep people coming back. There is just too much competition. You need to exceed your customers' expectations, every time. You serve one person at a time, and the more personal that interaction, the more you'll exceed their expectations, and the happier customers will be.

Here is a list of basic customer expectations and some hints on how to meet and/or exceed them. Your customers expect:

- **Quality first.** Price is secondary when the goal is quality, freshness, superior performance and taste.
- **First come, first serve.** It can be difficult during peak periods to keep track of who entered first, but don't let pushy customers or your inattention make someone wait any longer than absolutely necessary.
- **To pay quickly.** Be certain that your cash register is properly stocked to give change and manned by a well-trained person with cash-handling experience.
- **To know long it will take for gift-wrapping,** special orders or personalized products.
- **Your staff to know about the products you sell,** how equipment is used, the right tool for the job and some background information on vineyards, food producers, etc.
- **Your staff to care more about customers** than when the next break is or what they saw at the movies last night.

Do you know what your customers expect when they come through the door? Are you out to exceed those expectations and give each guest a memorable and delightful experience every time?

Ways to Delight

Customers are delighted when you care—it's as simple as that. Doing things that demonstrate how much you care will make a difference. Part of the trick here, however, is that there is no trick. You have to be sincere. People know when they're being treated with sincerity or with a mechanical technique. Sincerity works. Here is a list of practices that, when done with sincerity, can give customers a feeling of being taken care of, given real value or simply delighted. These touches may appear to customers to be extraordinary or creative—things that they never would have thought of themselves.

- **Umbrellas when it rains.** Keep an extra large umbrella handy to protect your customers while they carry bags to their cars.

- **Free stuff while they wait.** People don't mind waiting as much when they have a complimentary cookie and a glass of warm cider to keep them toasty. They will appreciate you going the extra mile.

- **A place to rest and wait.** Provide a couple of chairs for waiting. A bench or "ice cream" table outdoors also makes a nice place for people to rest or wait for others to finish shopping.

- **Introduce yourself.** People like to meet the person in charge. They appreciate that someone important is checking in on them.

- **Share "secrets" with them.** Have a new food item debuting next week? Why not give away free samples today to whet people's appetites? Don't forget to ask their opinion and give them a discount coupon for next week.

- **Free postcards and postage.** Do a lot of tourist business? Why not give them stamped postcards (depicting your store, of course) for sending their "Wish you were here" messages? It's a very low price to pay for something they'll appreciate and advertises your store all over the world.

- **Fax directions** to customers and provide mapping capabilities to your Web site. Have a great, clear map on hand, and when callers ask for directions to your store, offer to fax it to them.

- **Have the directions on your Web site.** You don't want them frazzled when they get to you, and you certainly don't want them unable to make it at all! If they don't have a fax or Internet access, make sure you can give them clear, explicit directions over the phone.

- **Create memories.** If you offer classes or "happy hour" tastings, have an instant camera on hand and snap a few shots for them to take home. If you intend on using any photos for store promotions or advertising, be certain to have attendees sign photo releases.

- **Display a guest book.** Make sure your customers fill in the guest book; you need a mailing list of your patrons for sending them promotional material. Try to collect birth dates and anniversaries for your database as well.

Word-of-Mouth Advertising

Positive word-of-mouth is the best advertising there is, without question. Does it just come by accident or only from having great service? Yes and no. Great word-of-mouth comes from your customers having something great to talk about and their sharing it effectively. Do you have a deliberate, creative and authentic plan in place to create great word-of-mouth? You can and should have everything to do with whether your customers have something to say and whether or not they're saying it.

Customers don't talk about you unless they're thinking about you. You want them thinking about you in the right way, which means you have to educate your customers on why they come to you. To do this, you must create points of difference between you and your competitors. Then people can tell their friends about your great selection of tea pots or how wonderful the jams are that you stock from Denmark.

An effective word-of-mouth program has five main goals:

1. Inform and educate your patrons.
2. Make the customer a salesperson for your store.
3. Give customers reasons to return.
4. Make your service unique and personal.
5. Distinguish your business from the competition.

Points of Difference

If you want your customers to return month after month and tell their friends and family about you, you need to distinguish yourself from the competition. You do this by creating "points of difference."

What is different about your establishment? your concept? your product choices? your atmosphere? Do you guarantee your service? give free coffee to waiting customers? have several organic choices? What makes your place memorable and different from the competition?

Find a memorable way to distinguish your store. Give your business a real identity and give your customers something to discuss with other potential customers.

Educating Customers on the Differences

Having a great idea in place is not enough; you have to tell your customers about it and give them the right words to pass it on.

Your customer tells his neighbor he got a chef's knife at your store.

- Your customer tells every one he found the top-rated German steel chef's knife at your store and he gets free sharpening for a lifetime!

Details differentiate your product and make yours the place to go for something extraordinary.

How do you get this information across? Arm your staff with words they can comfortably work into a conversation. Gourmet food, cooking equipment and tools all have a lingo. Your staff should understand the jargon and use it whenever appropriate (never to show-off or embarrass the less well-informed).

For example: You offer allergy-free products. When customers call to ask, say, "Dave's Kitchen Shoppe offers wheat-free alternatives. We're the only place in town that does."

An effective word-of-mouth program not only creates points of difference between you and the competition; it educates your customers on those distinctions. If you give your customers a great experience and the words to describe it, they'll talk about it to their friends. The first step is to educate your employees on these points. A good way to put together a list of these differences is during a staff meeting when ideas can be tossed about and descriptions created.

Your Staff Makes the Difference

Your store is made up of two things in the eyes of your customers: your products and your service staff. The quality of service your customers receive will determine their opinion of your store. Your employees are the ones who will delight your customers, give them things to talk about and provide the crucial personal connection. Your staff will execute most of your sales promotions and programs, educate your customers about what makes your store better than the one down the street and give your customers information they can pass on to their friends.

Your staff will treat your customers the same way you treat your staff. If you want your staff to be gracious, to listen and to delight your customers, you have to do the same for them.

- **Greet customers quickly.** Smaller stores allow you to personally greet people as they enter or browse.

- **Don't leave customers waiting alone at the register.** Waiting will negatively affect a customer's mood. Your store should be filled with warm thoughts and happy memories.

- **Make eye contact.** Don't stare at the door, the floor or the artwork on the wall. Clear your head, smile and pay attention.

- **Make sure you're fully tuned in when talking to customers.** Don't talk to them as you're flying by; it makes people feel unimportant, and no one likes that feeling.

- **Focus your energy on taking care of your customers,** making them happy, doing little things that exceed their expectations and generally making their experience as enjoyable as possible.

- **Encourage your customers' choices.** People can be strange about making decisions. The simple act on your part of telling them that you've used or tasted what they're buying can take away any anxiety they have about making a bad choice.

- **Tell the store staff good news.** Just like you need to be sensitive to the mood of your customers, be sensitive to the mood of the store crew. The cashiers don't want to hear about things just when they're wrong. Pass along good news and they will probably make it easier for you to take care of your customers.

- **Tell customers about specific events at your store and invite them.** This is a more effective way to let them know you would love for them to come back and to build a personal connection. It can be much more effective to invite customers to return for your special on Tuesdays than just to say "Thanks. Come again."

- **Show gratitude.** People are dealing with a lot in their lives and you have a chance to "make their day." Express gratitude in the tone of your voice when you thank them for their patronage or invite them to come back. Making them feel appreciated will make them remember you and the store.

- **Make personal recommendations.** Tell your customers what you like. This is not suggestive selling because it's sincere and, therefore, won't alienate your customers. Your enthusiasm will be infectious, even if customers don't buy what you recommend. It won't bother them that you're excited about what's on display.

How, as a manager, can you make it easiest for your staff to do these things? For one, have them taste the food you sell. Ideally, they should know how every item is made so they can speak knowledgably about it. Throw a tasting party where the staff gets to know each other and gets an education—then they will be able to make educated and sincere recommendations. Nothing is more persuasive than a fellow food lover who knows what he or she is talking about.

Also, let them use their own words to convey their enthusiasm. It's hard to make a personal recommendation using someone else's words. You want them sharing their enthusiasm, not a canned version of yours. Your crew will find their own way of expressing their enthusiasm. Letting them in on what you sell is the best way to give them something to be enthusiastic about!

Motivating Your Staff

How are you going to impart all this newfound wisdom and good spirit to your staff, and how are you going to get them excited about delighting your customers? You need an effective, uplifting staff meeting.

Most staff meetings are far from invigorating. In fact, they usually create an energy dip and a staff that feels like they are on management's bad side. An uplifting staff meeting is not just a gathering of bodies with one person giving out information; it generates a positive feeling within the entire group. An effective staff meeting has three main goals:

- Generating positive group feeling.
- Starting a dialogue.
- Training.

Positive Group Feeling

This will help your staff discover what it has in common and think in terms of working together, as opposed to strictly as individuals. Share good news in order to build good feeling. Staff meetings are not a good time to address individual or group shortcomings. Find the positive—even if you need to hunt for it—and talk about it. This is how you will build a supportive feeling and get people talking.

Dialogue

A good dialogue is a comfortable back-and-forth of ideas that gets people connected and leaves your staff feeling that they're a truly creative part of your store. You learn from the staff and they learn from you. Promoting this flow of ideas reduces the "Us vs. Them" mentality and reinforces team spirit. If everybody is on the same team, service improves while productivity and profits go up.

Training

Good staff meetings are places to share ideas for better performance. This is your chance to pass along tips to your staff while having them learn from each other. Your employees are intelligent people and they instinctively know what works. Encouraging them to share thoughts about work will turn staff meetings into a forum for discussing ideas. This atmosphere will dramatically improve their learning curve.

Ideally, you should hold a quick staff meeting before every shift every day to explain daily specials, discuss upcoming events and put everyone in a positive mood. Longer meetings should be scheduled "after hours" with ample time for discussions and learning (or reinforcing) important or complex topics (safety or sanitation issues, for example). Never sacrifice "actual" customer service to hold a meeting on improving customer service! Customers are priority #1.

If you frequently cancel staff meetings, it sends the message that they are not important and that the staff's opinions are equally unimportant. An effective pre-shift meeting should last no longer than 15 minutes. If it's longer, you may lose people's attention; shorter, you won't get enough said. Pick a length, and start and finish on time. Include the entire staff. This may be a good time to review today's specials or new products.

Possible Format for a 10–15 Pre-Shift Meeting:

Before you start, remember that the thing that most determines how your meeting will go is your own state of mind. Are you looking at your staff as a group of dedicated people, committed to doing a great job, or a bunch of goof-offs? Are you a coach on the playing field seeking to facilitate and encourage people's best performances, or a judge looking to identify and punish people's mistakes? Rest assured that however you approach the meeting, your staff will feel your mood and it will affect the work they do. Get committed to building on people's strengths and holding energizing staff meetings.

- **Good news (1–2 minutes).** Acknowledge what works and create a good mood. Find something about the business that shows people doing a good job and making customers happy. Acknowledge the doer or bearer of the news with sincerity.

- **Daily news (2–3 minutes).** Outline what's new and upcoming events.

- **Ask your staff (5 minutes).** This is the most important part of the meeting. This is your opportunity to find out what's really going on in your store and what people are thinking about. Listen. Don't interrupt with your own thoughts and don't judge people's comments.

  Create a safe space for people to sincerely share what's on their minds and to learn from each other.

  How well you listen directly affects how much they're willing to say. Since they are your store, as well as your access to the nitty-gritty, get them talking. If they're shy, ask them questions.
  - What's working for you?
  - What's making things tough?
  - Where have things broken down?
  - What questions from customers have you been unable to answer?

  Once you get the ball rolling, you may find it hard to stop. Good! That means people have things to say and you'll benefit.

  Asking the rest of the staff if they feel the same way as the speaker is a great way to see if there is a group sentiment and to gauge the size of the issue being presented.

- **Training (3–5 minutes).** If staff comments run over, let it cut into this time. It's important that your staff learn from you, but it's more important for you to learn from them. Plus, they will be more open to learning from you, if they know you're listening to them.

- Use this time to talk about a single point you want your staff to focus on during this shift, to give out specific knowledge about a product or to train in another targeted way. Focus is important. If you tell people how long the meeting will last and hold to that, they will give you their attention. If you go over, you'll lose their attention and their trust. Get to the point and trust that they got it.

Learning how to conduct productive staff meetings is worth your effort. Developing a good rapport with your employees will make everyone more successful—and your customers happier!

Focus on Making Your Customers Happy

If you dedicate your energies towards building an establishment where your staff are treated with respect and gratitude, they will treat you and your customers in the same way. Focus on building an environment that is friendly, helpful, informed and welcoming, and people will come back again and again. This can happen by taking the weight of sales off your staff's shoulders. Everybody—especially customers—should feel they are on the same page. People will give if they are given to and taken care of, and they will never come back if they feel taken advantage of.

Your job is to create a place that people think of first when looking for the newest electronic gadget or trendy spice—and that they tell their friends about. Again:

- Build customer loyalty.
- Dedicate your business to delighting your customers.
- Give your customers something to tell their friends about.
- Give customers incentives to return.
- Become connected. Your staff is your store. Become connected to your staff to help them connect with your customers.

9

Marketing Your Business

Build it and they will come might work in the movies but in the real world, it is a sure way to fail. Businesses without sufficient operating capital frequently cut their marketing budget first. That's because they see advertising as an expense instead of an investment in their business. Failing to advertise when times get tough may help your cash flow temporarily—but only until new customers stop seeking you out or occasional customers forget where you are located. Instead of cutting your advertising, you need to invest wisely!

Often when small businesses think of marketing, they think of the huge budgets that bombard us with soft drink commercials, Super Bowl ad launches and infomercials. Marketing is an all-encompassing term that means any activity you do that creates an image and recognition of yourself and your business and relays a message.

- When you dress for a date, you are marketing yourself.
- When you introduce yourself to a stranger, you are marketing yourself.
- When you support a charity, you are marketing yourself.
- When you sponsor a Little League team, you're marketing your business.
- When you decorate your store windows, you're marketing your business.
- When you hand out your business card, you're marketing your business.

Hiring Marketing Experts

Outsourcing your marketing to an advertising and/or public relations (PR) agency can be an excellent business investment. For an hourly rate, set fee and/or a percentage of your advertising purchases, a full-service agency can help you:

- Fashion your image—design a logo, mascot or visual message.
- Construct an advertising message—create a slogan that represents your business and reminds potential customers of what you do.
- Develop advertising campaigns—recommend the right media to reach your ideal customers.
- Produce print and electronic ads for newspaper, direct mail, magazines, TV, radio and the Internet.
- Create positive buzz—develop public relations activities.
- Make media buys—negotiate and purchase ad time or space.

As a small-business owner, your budget may restrict you from hiring a full-service advertising agency. Hiring an independent marketing consultant and freelance business communication writer can be a cost-effective alternative.

When hiring marketing experts, look for:

- Experience with retail and food service businesses.
- Smaller firms where you will be working with experienced marketers instead of underlings.
- Well-developed proposals.
- Willingness to work within your set budget.

Remember: Investing in the services of an advertising agency or marketing consultant can pay for itself. They can steer you away from costly mistakes, create a consistent message and negotiate lower ad rates.

Do-It-Yourself Marketing

Millions of entrepreneurs successfully advertise and promote their business. They make wise buying decisions, track their ads' effectiveness and grow their business. Conversely, others overspend on promotions that look unprofessional, fail to create a single image or message and, worst of all, don't increase your sales!

Should you handle your own marketing?

- Are you interested in learning about marketing?
- Is it a wise use of your time?
- Can you be objective?
- Can you handle aggressive ad salespeople?
- Do you have a creative eye?

As you can see from our examples above, marketing your business includes the details of daily business life. These are all your responsibility; however, more complex and costly marketing can be successfully handled in house also.

If you have no prior marketing experience, you can learn and implement practical ways to let people know about your business. Below are some resources to help you set your plan in motion.

- The U.S. Postal Service offers direct mail services and advice for small businesses. Visit their Web site at www.usps.com/grow/welcome.htm to learn more.

- Do-it-yourself e-mail marketing can be a great way to reach people. Constant Contact (www.constantcontact.com) provides user-friendly services. EmailFactory (www.emailfactory.com) and GotMarketing (www.gotmarketing.com) are other cost-effective e-mail services.

- Learn about specific marketing techniques at MarketIt Right (www.marketitright.com).

- Explore creative marketing ideas at Idea Site for Businesses (www.ideasiteforbusiness.com).

Guerilla Marketing

Marketing guru Jay Conrad Levinson is considered the father of Guerilla Marketing—a principle that empowers small businesses to become active marketers without breaking the bank. His various marketing and PR books, Web site (www.gmarketing.com) and business tools are filled with hands-on practical advice. Jay markets himself and Guerilla Marketing through free newsletters, radio programs, seminars and individual coaching. You can purchase his books at his Web site or your favorite bookseller.

As a small-business owner, you'll find these Guerilla Marketing books helpful.

- *Guerrilla Publicity*
- *Guerrilla Marketing Attack*
- *Guerilla Advertising*
- *Guerilla Marketing Excellence*

Desktop Publishing Applications and Ideas

There are hundreds of reasons to own and utilize a computer in your retail operation. The computer, if utilized effectively, will save you enormous amounts of time and money. Here are just a few ideas for desktop publishing. Print your own:

- Customer and/or employee newsletters
- Counter displays
- Discount coupons and customer gift certificates
- Direct mail flyers or postcards
- Menus
- Business cards
- Employee-of-the-month certificates
- Advertising posters
- Employee manuals
- Office stationery

If you are going to print your documents on your own laser or inkjet printer,

Microsoft Publisher® is a simple-to-learn program that includes templates and some basic artwork. Microsoft's Web site also has free enhancements for Publisher.

If you want more control and perhaps need to have a professional printer handle the finished design, Adobe PageMaker® is a full-featured desktop publisher, and the newest versions include an assortment of prepared templates for common items. You can use these templates in the provided color schemes and artwork, or modify them to suit your needs.

Beyond the basics of advertising and menu creation, we recommend hiring a graphic designer or printer with an in-house design staff. Don't spend unnecessary hours when they can create a professional presentation quickly. Doing it yourself has a point of diminishing returns—your time should be spent where it can make you the most money.

The Effective Use of E-Mail

E-mail, short for electronic mail, can be a convenient way to confirm orders with suppliers or send out coupons to customers. You can obtain an e-mail address from your Internet Service Provider or by registering a unique domain name. If you have an American Online account, your e-mail could be something like sweettreats@aol.com. A domain name is everything after the "@" sign on any e-mail address or after the "www" in a Web address.

Do I Need a Web Site?

In a word, "Yes"! Each day, millions of people around the globe use the Internet for work, play, shopping and research. Your business will be visible to everyone from your neighbor to a French homemaker to a Japanese farmer.

Perhaps your goal is to offer the latest food trend ingredients in your city or to carry elegant handmade stemware, so why would you care about visibility beyond your community? Because the world shrinks every day and the possibilities are unlimited—in whom you can reach, what you can sell or who will find their way to your door. No other marketing tool can provide such comprehensive coverage for such a nominal investment.

Your Web site is your full-color brochure where you can tell people:

- **Who you are**—Tools for the home chef.
- **What you make**—We specialize in superior quality culinary equipment and tools.
- **Who you serve**—Serving Old Town San Diego since 1988.
- **Where you are located**—At the corner of Red Hill and Spruce.
- **When you are open**—Open 9:30 a.m. to 7:00 p.m., Monday through Saturday.
- **Why they should buy from you**—Not just tools, but the best tools for the discriminating cook.
- **How to place your special order**—Use our online order system and your special order will be waiting for you!

The Internet offers marketing benefits beyond those of a print brochure. Your site can:

- **Be updated quickly without any "waste."** You don't have signs or flyers to toss when you introduce a new food item. Make their mouths water with beautiful pictures!
- **Be your electronic catalog.** Order your Christmas cookie cutters today!
- **Grow it as you grow.** It can be whatever size you want.
- **Be interactive,** where people are given a chance to respond directly to your information.
- **Have lasting value.** You can share cake-serving techniques and how to brew the perfect cup of tea.

- **Build community spirit.** You can announce and run charity events through your site, promote community activities, provide a community forum.

- **Sell your specialties** to "foodies" around the globe with e-commerce features.

Your Web site can also be a great way to communicate with your employees. A password-protected section can feature a company newsletter, explain benefits or post work schedules.

Reaching customers within your own community can also be done on the Web via digital cities, online city guides and other food or community-oriented sites where you can place an advertisement, free directory listing or link your Web site. Chambers of commerce, virtual travel guides, online wedding planner services and guide sites such as About.com (www.about.com).

Use the following checklist of potential advantages and see for yourself. Place a checkmark next to each advantage that would serve your business:

- ❑ Reach a global market.
- ❑ Gather marketing information.
- ❑ Analyze and evaluate marketing information.
- ❑ Generate additional sales.
- ❑ Establish more frequent and meaningful communication with customers and employees.
- ❑ Broadcast press releases.
- ❑ Submit invoices and expenses more quickly.
- ❑ Identify and solicit prospective employees.
- ❑ Provide immediate access to your catalog.
- ❑ Establish contact with potential "strategic partners" worldwide.
- ❑ Permit customers to place orders electronically.
- ❑ Reduce costs of goods sold through reduced personnel.

What to Put on Your Web Site

What kind of information can a retail store put on the Web? Remember that the site should reflect your store's personality. If you think of your store as classically elegant, then your site should have that appearance. If your store's décor is bright yellow and playful, then your site should have yellow accents and have a playful feel. Here are some ideas of what you can include on your business Web site.

- **A picture is truly worth a thousand words.** Don't just tell them you sell five kinds of salt—show them! You can show them: how inviting your store is, gift ideas for the budding chef, your cheerful staff at work, how you make the delicate frosting flowers with supplies from your store, racks of popular cookbooks and shelves of brightly colored dishes and ideas for special holiday meals.

- **News, events and specials.** Develop a Web-based newsletter to share your exciting news.

- **Directions.** Have a link to Mapquest.com right on your site. Customers enter their address, and they get door-to-door directions from their home to your store.

- **History.** Every town has a history. If your store or your building has an interesting history, share your story.

- **Area attractions.** Sell your store and your local community to the Web site visitor.

The opportunities are endless. Be imaginative!

Setting Up an Effective Web Site

You can build it yourself or you can hire an experienced Web development company. Microsoft FrontPage® provides convenient templates for the beginning Web designer. However, remember that just because a program is convenient, doesn't mean that you should spend your time becoming a Web designer.

You would need a unique domain name if you want to have your own Web site. To determine whether your store can be used as a dot com (.com) or dot net (.net), visit the Whois database of Web names at Network Solutions (www.networksolutions.com/en_US/whois/index.jhtml). Due to the tremendous growth of the Web, you may find your business name is already registered as a dot com. Try the dot net extension also. Variations such as adding your city name may be available. Avoid long names as they are hard to put on a business card and even harder for people to remember. Dashes should likewise be avoided as they can be confusing. Once you have found an available name, you can register it at Network Solutions (www.network-solutions.com) or one of the many registration companies on the Web. Fees vary so shop around and beware of companies that don't allow you to register yourself as the "owner" and as the "administrator."

When you have registered your domain name, it needs to be "pointed" somewhere on the Web. Some registration companies offer "free" camping until you have a Web site set up with a hosting company. You can create unique e-mail addresses such as bettybaker@sweettreats.com or orderdept-@kitchentreasures.com. Using different e-mail addresses on advertising can be a good way to tell how people found out about your store and the effectiveness of a specific ad campaign.

Remember that:

- **Your site must look professional.** A "homemade" site can reflect poorly on your business.
- **Your site must "work."** The mechanics behind the site and the navigational system are what makes it a pleasant visit for your customers and potential customers. Broken links or hard-to-operate ordering systems are real turn-offs.
- **Your site needs to be search-engine friendly.** Since 75 percent of all online active comes from finding a site via a search engine, your site must be easy to find. Your design and keyword-filled copy are important components.

- **Your site needs sales-oriented copy.** If words fail you, you'll need a copywriter, or at the very least someone with a flair for writing and excellent grammar and spelling skills.

- **Your time may be better spent on other store activities.** Avoid the entrepreneur trap of taking on too many tasks. Do what you do best and hire others to support you!

Hiring Web Pros

You may decide to hire professionals to design your Web site.The Internet is a good place to begin to find the right Web developer for your business. First, search for "web design [your city name]" to find locals who can handle the job. Following are some tips that will help you create he Web site you desire:

- **Look at other store sites.** If you see one that you like, contact the Webmaster (usually listed at the bottom of the page) and ask who created their site.

- **Make note of the retail store sites you visit.** Share what you like and what you don't with your Web designer.

- **Review Web developer portfolios and site samples.** Are they attractive? Do they function properly? Are they filled with annoying sounds and whizzing pictures? Do you know immediately upon visiting the site what they do?

Some Words of Caution

- **Don't overlook the little details.** Web users have become more perceptive and have bigger expectations—even for a local retail store site.

- **Invest your time and money wisely.** There is always a point of diminishing returns and inflated expectations.

- **Build a site that can grow with you.**

- **Keep in mind the "hidden costs."** Most developers don't include Web site hosting, domain-name registration and renewal, support and continued development services after site completion.

- **Make sure you promote your site.** A site is worthless if no one knows it exists. Search-engine registration is a critical part of a successful Web site.

A well-constructed Web site is an investment, not an expense. Integrate it with your newspaper, phone directory and other offline advertising efforts to maximize its returns. Don't forget to include your Web address on business cards, stationery, store packaging and radio ads; anywhere your customers might see or hear your name.

Find Support with Suppliers

Suppliers can also be a huge ally in promoting your business. Ask about what marketing programs and sales tools they have available for your use. Manufacturers often have co-op advertising programs where dollars are available for promoting the use of their products by your business. These funds can be used to create local PR campaigns and advertising in exchange for mentioning the company brand names. To locate co-op programs and confirm your eligibility, speak with wholesalers, distributors and other vendors about all available programs. Be aware: these "gifts" come with rules and regulations. Be certain to read them carefully, document your eligibility and keep good records.

Some publications (telephone books, directories, small newspapers, etc.) will provide creative services when you purchase an ad. This can save money; however, you may have limited control over the design and your ad may end up looking just like everyone else's.

Band Together

Another practical way to share the cost of advertising is to create an association of complementary businesses to produce omnibus ads. You can gather together businesses in your neighborhood, mall or business center; create a network of other "food" businesses such as a gourmet cook shop, a produce market, a wine store and a fish market. The businesses can be close for "walk-in" campaigns or located around town with similar customer demographics.

- Share the cost of a ½-page newspaper ad with other businesses in your strip mall or with other non-competitive food or home décor providers. Dividing the cost is frequently less expensive than purchasing your "share" separately.
- Create in-store promotions for each other. Think of create ways to cross-market your ad partners' products and they do the same for your store in their shops.
- Develop a punch card frequent-buyer program with an ad partner.
- Provide the refreshments or service for open houses and other special events. Create an attractive display and always have a sign that holds business cards.
- Hold a "sidewalk" sale with neighboring businesses. Provide food samples, plenty of seating and discount coupons to encourage people to return to your retail store later.

Your local chamber of commerce and other business associations are great resources for connecting with and building your marketing network.

Investing in Customers

So how much should you spend to acquire a new customer? There is no exact right or wrong answer. The key is to compare this cost against the lifetime value of a customer. If a new customer came in, bought a wooden spoon and never came back, no matter how little you spent on advertising, it would be a poor investment. If you spend $850 on a newspaper ad to find three new good customers, you'd recover that investment in the second month. However, even spending significantly more per customer can also be a wise investment with some profitable long-term rewards. In the example below, we look at these three "ideal" customers and their lifetime value. You'll soon see why customer retention is so important.

Lifetime Value

Let's use a simple example to help you realize the potential value of three different customers.

CUSTOMER LIFETIME VALUE ASSESSMENT				
3 Typical Customers	**Monthly**	**Annually**	**5 Years**	**15 Years**
Olivia Spencer is a personal chef interested in time-saving tools and cooking equipment.	$32	$384	$1,920	$5,760
Karen Stewart and her husband Ron love to cook. Karen stops by once a month for items such as spices, tools and wine.	$65	$780	$3,900	$11,700
Cameron Jeffries and Bill Tracy love to entertain. They stop by every Friday after work to stock up on imported olives, vinegars, jams, wine and fun serving utensils.	$378	$4,536	$22,680	$68,040
	$475	$5,700	$28,500	$85,500

The $850 you spend to acquire these three customers would be repaid many times over the year and following years. Of course, you will spend additional monies throughout the years in customer retention (bonuses, freebies, thank-you items, customer newsletters) so your true return wouldn't be quite as dramatic; but from the examples you can see why advertising can be a great investment.

Calculating Your Customer Acquisition Cost

If you are a new business, every customer is new and you'll know your advertising costs spent to bring customers in initially. (In other words, you won't have any prior activities to factor in.) At the end of your first 30 days of business, divide your customer count (assume individual transactions) by your actual advertising expenses[2] from pre-opening to the end of the 30-day cycle. In subsequent months, you'll compare the next 30 days with the prior. After a year, you'll be able to compare one 30-day period to the same period in the prior year. Some people use 13-month cycles for these calculations to give them results that are more accurate.

If you are taking over someone else's operation, you'll have the prior owner's financial data to use as a benchmark. If they did not keep detailed records, you can use some sales per customer factors to estimate the customer acquisition cost benchmark. To follow are some resources and tips on calculating your customer acquisition cost.

- These assumptions don't take into account the residual benefit you receive from the prior owner's good reputation along with prior and ongoing word-of-mouth advertising, PR or formal advertising.
- Data gathered on a daily and/or monthly basis must be compared to like periods.
- Haley Marketing Group offers a lifetime value of a customer calculator at www.haleymarketing.com/c_calc.html.

The purpose of this exercise goes beyond decision-making and budgeting; it should also help you feel more comfortable in investing in solid, long-term advertising campaigns. In addition, recognizing the long-term value of a customer reinforces the wisdom of giving a customer a free cake to satisfy a problem. Your cost of $6 is just a fraction of what they give you!

[2] You should allocate a percentage of your annual advertising buys over the 12-month accounting cycle. If you purchase a $1,000 ad in July but it doesn't appear in print until September, the expense would be used in September's calculations. In other words, use the publication/air date as opposed to contract or payment dates. To learn more about the value of a customer and how much to spend on advertising, visit HTMail at www.htmail.com/article3.html.

Customer Investment

During your first month of operation, your "new customer" data would be everyone who visits. However, differentiating between new and repeat customers can be difficult. If all your business were custom, one-to-one sales, you'd easily tally who is new and who is a repeat customer. However, a typical retail outlet will have to make estimates and assumptions.

The basic formula for computing your customer acquisition cost is your total advertising costs divided by the number of new customers. Let's say you spent $800 in June (not your first month) and the number of individual sales (your customers) rose by 100 from the prior June. Your June cost to acquire 100 new customers is $8. In the real world, you may have only had 25 new customers. However, your great products, excellent service and ongoing advertising meant that you rang up an extra 75 sales!

Advertising

Advertising is a direct activity where you purchase time or space to present your message. You purchase time for cable TV ads or radio spots and space for newspaper display ads or a Web site. Advertising is often a broad activity where you reach out to a huge audience in hope of capturing the attention (and money) of a few potential customers. There are two major factors you'll use to calculate your advertising return on investment (ROI). The first is the number of potential customers you reach, and the second is the acquisition cost of each new customer.

The Most Eyes

The more people who see your ad, the less expensive it is per "potential" customer. This is a simple way of looking at the value of your ads. Calculating your advertising's cost per "potential" customer can be done by:

- Dividing the number of impressions of your potential audience (impressions means copies printed, viewings are for visual mediums such as billboards, the Web and listeners for radio) by the cost for the ad.

- An example: You purchase a small ad in the local community newspaper for $100. Their circulation is 10,000. Divide $100 by 10,000 for a $.01 cost per impression.

- Compare that with: you purchase a regional magazine ad for $800. Their circulation is 200,000. Divide $800 by 200,000 for a $.004 cost per impression.

- Assuming all other factors (demographics, distribution, etc.) were equal, the best value is the magazine ad.

- However, by factoring in demographics and ability to reach your ideal customer, you'll come up with a more accurate ad value. You want to reach people who have the financial resources to afford your products and the interest to purchase them.

Acquisition Costs

By selecting advertising that targets your ideal customer demographics, you'll increase your success rate. The more people you connect with that match your "ideal customer" profile, the more cost-effective your advertising. Advertise where they most likely will see you—whether that is your city entertainment guide or a local health magazine. A $100 ad that brings in one customer has a $100 per-customer cost. However, a $1,000 ad that reaches 55 new customers costs you just over $18 each.

Your Advertising Effectiveness

For a retail operation, it can be very difficult to figure out which advertising brought in new customers. Did they find you in the Yellow Pages or see your newspaper ad? You need to build in ways to gather this information into your campaigns whenever possible. Without knowing how they found you, it becomes more difficult to eliminate the non-productive advertising and increase the productive types. Below are a few ways to see which ads are working for you:

- Ask your customers how they found you.
- Provide a form on your Web site for customers to fill out.
- Over the counter, periodically have staff ask people as they ring up their order. Keep a simple running tally.
- Include a postage-paid reply card when packaging orders.
- Include a reply card that, when brought back completed, they get a discount or freebie.
- Ask and record when taking phone or face-to-face custom orders.
- Set up automatic data gathering mechanisms. Use unique e-mail addresses and unique phone numbers for specific promotions.
- Coupons with codes indicating when and where they where printed and/or distributed.

Taking time to learn what ads are drawing best will help you make critical budgeting decisions. You won't have to assume that your billboards are working when in fact it is the door hangers.

What Makes an Effective Ad?

A print or electronic ad is effective if it:

- Brings in more customers.
- Reminds customers to return.
- Increases your sales per customer.

Your ad might be clever, entertaining or educational, but unless you are increasing sales, you're wasting your time and money.

Some Ads Take Time

Some ads bring people into your store immediately; others plant a seed for future reference. You will be attracting three types of customers: 1) those with an ongoing need for your product (a weekly bottle of wine), 2) those with a special need (a holiday or birthday), and 3) true "foodies" interested in all things food will want to scope out your store for future reference. By adding a sense of urgency to your ads, you'll bring in the first group. The second group fits into the future reference category, unless your ad just happens to appear when they are ready to buy. The third group may drop by for a "get to know you" visit. If you do a good job in presenting impulse items, you'll capture a sale. This group just cannot resist trying a new food or buying a new tool. This third group has lasting value, so connect with them quickly and create a reason to return. Newsletters (e-mail or print), sales flyers and preferred customer promotions are well-received by this group.

To add a sense of urgency to your advertising:

- Always include an end date for all offerings. For ads that are on TV, radio or newspapers, the special should end in a week or less. For magazines with a longer "shelf life," a 30-day or longer offer would be more appropriate. Always be aware of print and pull dates. You'll turn off potential customers if your offer expired before the magazine was removed from the newsstand.

- Include a call to action. Tell them to drop by today, to bring in the coupon, to check out your Web site, to try your sample and register to win!

Repetition, Repetition, Repetition

Opt for a greater frequency—it is better to choose a smaller-sized ad that appears more often than a big ad that never is repeated. Many advertising experts believe that it takes 3 to 7 times of being exposed to your offer before people make a purchasing decision. You can vary your ads somewhat, but keep them consistent in visuals and message.

Your customers have busy lives, so keeping your name visible will remind them that they want to stop by and see what you have on sale. You'll also remind customers that they haven't stopped in for a while to see what's new.

Sell Benefits, Not Features

Sure, you may be the best store in four counties, but telling people that is more about your needs than theirs. Your advertising should be about how people benefit from your products. Many ads are just a list of all the things a business offers—these are the features. A good copywriter can help you transform these facts into reasons for your customers to buy.

FEATURES & BENEFITS	
Feature	**Benefit**
Open 7 days a week	Convenient hours for busy cooks.
All-natural ingredients	A healthier choice than preservative-filled…
Near Highway 5	Transform tonight's dinner in just 10 minutes…
All the best brands	We've done all the research so you can have the best tool for the job.
Telephone orders welcome	Save time by calling us before you leave the office.
Treats	Even busy lives deserve holiday treats.

Advertise Like a Pro

As you learn how to advertise and promote your business, you'll need to focus in on the mediums and messages that work. Here are some additional tips to get you going:

- In radio ads, repeat your message and call to action at the end of the spot to reinforce it.
- Give people directions that are easy to follow or provide a map. This

is especially important if you aren't located on a heavy traffic route.

- Don't assume people know what you mean; use common consumer terms, but don't talk down to people.

- Build in ways to monitor responses.

- Be consistent—in message and visual presentation. Use the same slogan repeatedly and always include your exact logo to build recognition.

- Make your advertising ideas relevant. Great visuals are important, but don't forget the sales message.

- Choose advertising that brings in customers over PR such as sponsoring a basketball team. Every business has a budget, so put your money in customer acquisition first—then public relations.

- If you cannot directly associate business growth with a campaign, discontinue it. Your goal is sales and profits!

10

Public Relations: How to Get Customers in the Door

Public relations (PR) are really the sum of its many definitions. It's the message a person, company or organization sends to the public. It's a planned effort to build positive opinions about your business through actions and communications about those actions. In short, it's any contact your organization has with another human being and the resulting opinion. This opinion may or may not be accurate, but it comes from everything the public reads, sees, hears and thinks about you. Effective PR has been described as becoming a positive member of your community (and getting credit for it).

PR should be part of your overall marketing communications program. This includes advertising, internal communications and sales promotion. Speeches, contests, promotions, personal appearances and publicity are parts of PR, but really, the results generated from all of these parts—including acquiring unpaid-for media space and time—are PR. It's who the public thinks you are and the nurturing of that opinion in a positive way.

What PR Does (and Doesn't Do) for You

If done well, PR distinguishes you from the pack in the eyes of your customers. It leaves them with a favorable impression of you and great tidbits of information to pass on to their friends about your establishment. It makes you newsworthy in a great way and can help save your reputation and standing in your community during an emergency.

Good PR improves sales by creating an environment in which people choose to spend their time and money. As said before, PR is getting credit for being an upstanding member of your community. If you are not, PR can't make you look like you are. PR accentuates the positive and creates lasting value by highlighting what makes your establishment special. PR cannot create lasting value if none is there to begin with. What it can do is communicate existing value effectively, so it lives in your customers' minds.

Good PR can make a good story great, and a bad story less bad. However, PR is not just the public's opinion of your business; it's also the physical state of your establishment. People aren't just interacting with your staff; they're interacting with your facility. If the media are reporting on something wonderful that happened at your store, but the place is in a state of disrepair, what are you communicating about your establishment?

The key to implementing an effective PR campaign is determining what your business's image is, what you want it to be and how best you can create that image in the eyes of the public. You need to clearly define your objectives and create a plan that will implement them. PR is not a way to gloss over a tarnished image or to keep the press at a safe distance; it's an organized and ongoing campaign to accentuate the positives of whom you truly are.

PR is Different from Advertising

PR is not advertising; PR uses advertising as one of its tools. A good PR campaign is almost always coordinated with advertising, but PR is not paid-for time and space. In advertising, clients pay the media to carry a message and the client has complete control over this message. With PR, the media receives no money. Because of this, your story about the famous movie star dropping by your store may end up on the 5 o'clock news, buried in the back of your local newspaper or nowhere at all. The success of a PR story often depends on how timely it is or whether an editor feels it's worth reporting on. Furthermore, only a portion of your intended message may be used. The media may not even use your store's name. Because they are choosing to write about your topic, and you've basically given them only a potential idea for a story, the story could end up in a very different form than you initially presented or hoped.

PR doesn't give you the control you have with advertising. However, when done well, it garners positive attention for your establishment, is hugely cost-effective and is more credible than advertising. This is because the public is getting its information from a third party—not directly from a business. Customers assume advertising to be self-serving, but a positive message delivered by a third party is perceived to be authentic and trustworthy. Third-party messages are infinitely more persuasive than advertising.

The Marriage of PR and Marketing

Public relations are one of the crucial aspects of a successful marketing plan. When management is communicating effectively with customers, employees and community leaders, it is implementing an effective marketing plan. Fundamentally, all marketing is integrated. Consumers don't distinguish between one message from your business and another—all the messages are yours. In that light, since it's your job to communicate as well as possible, understanding that all your marketing is integrated allows you to focus on an overall approach to building good PR.

Launching a PR Campaign

In a small store, the manager may be solely responsible for public relations. In a larger establishment, the director of marketing or sales often plays this role. Having a single person designated as media liaison makes it simple for the press to get their questions answered and makes it much easier for you to control the flow of information to them. This back-and-forth is a critical element in your PR campaign. Once this liaison is determined, notify your staff. Advise them not to talk with the press, but to refer all media inquiries to your liaison.

Start Your PR Campaign Now

Public relations campaigns for a new business or new ownership of an existing business should start before your doors are open. Start by creating buzz within the community.

- Post "Coming Soon" signs.
- Look for complementary businesses (vendors, neighbors, banks, peers) to share the PR costs.
- Contact local media for business-oriented PR (business article in the newspaper).

In launching your campaign, it's important to remember that you will be competing with professionals for a very limited amount of airtime and/or editorial space. Reading newspapers and trying to determine which pieces were inspired by PR people—and what made editors choose them—is a good discipline. In addition, many community colleges offer courses in small-business public relations. The more expertise you have, the more effective your campaign will be.

If your establishment is part of a franchise, PR assistance may be available from the franchiser. If you manage an independent property, PR help may be available from your local Better Business Bureau, chamber of commerce or convention/visitors' bureau. Your local chapter of SCORE (www.score.org) offers advice on how to launch your PR program. An excellent resource for do-it-yourself PR and marketing is guru Jay Conrad Levinson's Guerilla Marketing® books, radio programs and Web site (www.gmarketing.com).

How to Apply Your PR Plan

Once you have established the objectives of your PR campaign and integrated them into your marketing plan, it is time to execute. These questions can help you do just that:

- What's the right medium for this strategy?
- Who are the key contacts?
- How strong are the necessary personal relationships required for this plan? Do any of these relationships need to be established or reestablished?
- Is this plan thorough? Have we considered all the downside risks?
- Are we prepared to deliver a press kit to selected media contacts?

This press kit is an essential part of your plan. It contains background information, newsworthy facts, contacts and phone numbers—all the pertinent information that will inform the media and direct them to you.

The press may not use one word of your materials, but there is a much greater likelihood they'll describe you the way you want them to if you've given them the resources to do just that.

When providing the press with information (spoken or written) be:

- **Honest.** The media want credible, honest material and relationships. Your message should be genuine and factual. This doesn't mean you have to reveal confidential data; it just means that your materials should be thorough and truthful.
- **Upfront.** Don't lie, dodge or cover up. If you don't have an answer to every question—and you might not—don't say "no comment," or "that information is unavailable." Simply respond that you don't have that information, but will provide it as soon as humanly possible. Then provide it as soon as humanly possible.

- **Factual.** Give the facts and follow up. If you supply the media with a printed handout of key facts, it greatly lessens the chances of your being misquoted. Make a concentrated effort to follow up and review information with the media. Again, if you don't have a requested piece of information, get it and follow up with a note and/or call to make sure the correct data reaches the media.

- **Concise.** The media is more apt to burn you for what you say, not what you don't. Be deliberate about providing the facts without editorializing, exaggerating or pulling things out of thin air.

- **Professional.** If you follow the above steps, you're on your way to building a strong and lasting relationship with the press. These relationships can sour instantly if you are reactionary, hostile, aloof, hypersensitive or argumentative in any way. No matter what you think of an interviewer, treat him or her with respect, courtesy and professionalism. Causing negative reactions from the press will deny you print space and airtime.

How you interact with the press is crucial, but it's only half the process. The content of what you communicate to them—having a clear and deliberate focus about how you are going to tell your story—is the other side of press relations. The following list will help you identify your purpose and communicate it effectively to the press:

- **Identify your purpose.** Why do you want public exposure? To what are you specifically trying to draw attention? Are you selling your store's expansion? Then don't go on about its famous muffins. Be sure you are conveying your purpose.

- **Identify your target.** Who are you targeting? Prospective customers? Your employees? The local business community? Civic leaders? Lay out whom you want to reach, and then determine who in the media will speak to them most effectively.

- **Look at it from the media's viewpoint.** Why would this be interesting to the media? Figure out how your interests can be packaged in a way that directly matches the press's interests. Make your story one they want to print; that is, one that will help them sell papers, gain listeners, etc.

- **Customize your materials.** Once you have identified your purpose, who your target is and the media's angle, tailor your materials to include all three. Give the press everything they need to tell the story—photos, copy, etc.—and be sure it's in exactly the style and medium they're using.

- **Know where to send your materials.** Is your story a business story or a feature story? Do you know the difference? A business story goes to your newspaper's business section editor. Feature stories go to the appropriate editor: food, community, lifestyle, etc. It's a very good idea to cultivate relationships with these editors beforehand so that when the time arises, they are thinking well of you and would like to help.

- **Make their jobs easy.** Do not ask the media for the ground rules for getting press and building relationships—learn these on your own and then meet them. Spending valuable time and resources building a relationship with a reporter, only to then submit materials at the last minute or give them insufficient or inaccurate information, burns bridges quickly. Do as much of their work for them as possible: give them something that is ready to go, answers all their questions and is interesting. This is the difference between staying in the middle and rising to the top of a busy person's in-box. Also, be available immediately to answer questions. If a reporter calls and you aren't there or don't return the call immediately, your great story—prepared at considerable expense—may end up in the trash.

Before you begin your media campaign, you should get to know the media as much as possible. This may mean inviting them—one at a time—for a brief tour of your establishment and, perhaps, an afternoon tea. This gives them a connection to you and your business and begins to build a relationship.

These visits are not the time to sell them on doing a story on you. It's a time for you to get to know each other and to build a relationship. If the reporters trust you, they will help you, and vice versa. They need article ideas as much as you need press, and getting to know them will give you insight into how you can help them do their job. A secondary goal is that you will be establishing yourself as a gourmet food expert. When they need a quote or some advice, you'll be the one they call!

Once your friends in the media trust you won't be barraging them with endless story ideas, you can begin your media campaign. It is important to remember that having a positive rapport with a reporter doesn't mean he or she will do a story on you. Your relationship with the reporter will help get a newsworthy story printed, but you won't get a boring story to press just because the reporter likes you. Your story needs to be newsworthy on its own. In addition, reporters are always working against the clock. The more you can give them pertinent, accurate, concise information, the better your chances of getting their attention.

If you've built a respectful relationship with the media, a reporter who gets a story from an interview or news conference at your establishment will mention your place in his or her story. These are the "freebies" that come from developing strong relationships with the media and learning to think in their terms.

Many businesses go one step further and give their media contacts news releases that are written in journalistic style. A news release describes the newsworthy development in your store in a ready-to-print article. Editors can then change it or print it as is. These can be immensely valuable for getting your message out there.

If writing journalistic articles is beyond your reach or budget, tip sheets can be very effective in getting your story across. A tip sheet gets the message to the media by simply outlining the who, what, when, where, why and how of your story. It's basically an outline of the story the reporter will then write. Tip sheets give the spine of the story and, because they are so concise, often get more attention from busy editors.

Here are a few more tips on how to work effectively with the media:

- Earn a reputation for dealing with the facts and nothing else.
- Never ask to review a reporter's article before publication.
- Never ask after a visit or an interview if an article will appear.

- Follow up by phone to see if your fact sheet or press release has arrived, if the reporter is interested and if he or she needs anything else.

- Provide requested information—photos, plans, etc.—A.S.A.P.

Creating Your Press Kit

It may be a good idea to hire a part-time PR consultant, former reporter or editor who can help you present your materials to the press. If this is beyond your budgetary limits, the following is a list of essentials for creating your own Press Kit.

- **Fact sheet.** One of the most helpful items of media information, the fact sheet does most of the reporter's research for him or her. It also shortens the length of interviews by answering questions in advance. It should describe your business and what you are trying to get press for. At a glance, it tells where you are located, when you opened, your food offerings, specialties and number of employees. It should also specify the types of facilities you have, such as historical information on the building and what type of atmosphere your store has (family friendly or upscale singles).

- **Staff biographies.** You will need to write biographies for all of your key executives. These list work experience, education, professional memberships, honors and awards. Include information on ties to the community and other human-interest angles.

- **Good photography.** Do not take chances with an amateur photographer. Space is very limited in the print media, and editors go through thousands of photographs to choose just a few. This is true even for local editors. Don't give them any reason to ignore your pictures. Have them taken by a pro. Ask for references and check them thoroughly. When the photos are done, write an explanatory caption for each picture in your collection. This gives editors an easy understanding of what they're looking at. Then, before sending photos to the media, be sure you find out whether they prefer black and white, slides, transparencies, etc., and send them in the desired format.

- **Press kit folder.** Put all of these materials into a single folder with your store's name and logo on the cover. You might also include brochures, a brief on your involvement with local charities, etc. Don't overstuff it, but give the press a solid idea of what distinguishes you from the competition. Do not include press clippings. You'll diminish your newsworthiness. No respectable editor/reporter wants to rehash something that has already been done. The rare exception to this might be that your store was featured on the cover of a national food magazine and your news angle is "Local Retail Store Receives National Recognition."

What's News?

Once you have identified your target media and begun your media relations program, you need to learn what makes news. To do this, pick up the paper, and turn on the TV. The media is looking for the strange, volatile, controversial and unusual. It's not newsworthy that you run a nice retail store that provides unique foodstuffs at a reasonable price. It's newsworthy when a customer gets food poisoning at your store. This is not the type of news you want to make, but is it news. Obviously, you want to be making great news. One of the foundations of this is taking steps to avoid negative articles: making sure your food safety measures and sanitation ratings are excellent, your staff treats customers courteously, etc.

Once you've taken these steps, you are ready to generate positive stories in the media. How? Well, what do editors find newsworthy? Here is a list of basic newsworthiness criteria:

- Is it local?
- Is it timely?
- Is it unique, unusual, strange?
- Does it involve and affect people?
- Will it evoke human emotion?

Think in terms of what it is that sets your establishment apart from the competition and what is newsworthy about those qualities. When this is done, again, target your media. When you have a story, be smart about who would be interested in writing about it and whose audience would love to read about it. Here is a short list of possibly newsworthy ideas:

- A new manager or exclusive distributorship of a product.
- Visits by well-known chefs, teacher/lecturers, cookbook authors, wine experts, politicians, entertainers, authors or local heroes.
- Hosting a charitable event, sponsoring a school activity, feeding the hungry.
- Personal stories about the staff: an employee who returned a doctor's medical bag, helped a patron stop choking, foiled a robbery, etc.

Choosing Your PR Contacts

The first goal in building strong media relations is to determine who your target media are. News media should be classified by the audiences they reach and the means they use to carry their messages. Your target media will change according to the type of message you wish to send and the type of audience you wish to reach.

Once you know who your target is, the next task is to build a media list. This list includes names of appropriate editors, reporters, news directors, assignment editors, media outlets, addresses and contact numbers, along with demographic information. If you already have an advertising agency, they can either assist you with PR or refer you to a skilled consultant to handle the task. The agency can also gather and interpret PR statistical data for you. However, most small businesses won't have the budget to hire a PR firm so the task is left to management.

If you want to mail fact sheets, press releases, press kits, etc., you can hire a company that sells media mailing lists, and you can pay them or another firm to do your mailing for you. If that is beyond your budget, you'll need to spend some research time creating your own list. If you are handling your own publicity, you'll have to do some Web research and/or telephone work to find the right person within each organization.

Start by calling the editorial department of a newspaper or a newsroom will get you the contact numbers of the people you seek to reach. Your assigned advertising rep for the TV, radio, newspaper or magazine may be able to direct you to appropriate editorial staff people.

Your first call should be to the food editor of your local paper. Mentions in a column, a recipe for a home baker or how-to articles are valuable ways to create great "buzz" about your business. The business editor wants to know about your business skills, sales techniques, expansion efforts or technical advances within your business. The lifestyle editor wants to know about your leadership, charitable and good citizen activities. The community/neighbor editor is interested in the local angle.

Magazines, radio and TV stations will have similar editorial managers, each with their own responsibilities and agendas. Your job is to find these people and to tailor your news information to their needs.

In addition, you may want to target national media, as well as specialized trade and business publications. Online publications and Web sites dealing with food-related topics (trade and consumer) can also be a way to get your name out to the public.

Developing Allies

During your campaign, it's also important that you search for allies. Allies are businesses and organizations that have similar goals to yours. Your state's Tourism/Travel Promotion Office can be a great resource for this. This office is working year-round to bring business and leisure customers to your state. These, of course, are also your prospective customers if you specialize in regionally unique foods. Your state's travel promotion officials will be happy to give you advice on how to tie in with their advertising, PR and other promotional programs.

Most states also have a Business/Economic Development Department that will be happy to help you, since their goal is to create new business in your state. Their mailing list will keep you informed of planned promotions. When meeting with state officials, it's a good idea to volunteer to assist their promotional and PR programs. Doing this gets you "in the loop" and, often, ahead of your competition, because you'll know about the programs your state is developing. There are a number of national travel industry organizations that work privately to generate travel in the United States. Hospitality and food service associations can also prove to be valuable allies, since they either have PR people on staff or use national PR agencies.

Locally, your chamber of commerce, convention center or tourism department may organize familiarization trips to your area. These are trips for travel writers and travel agents that showcase the attributes of your area. Let the organization arranging the introduction trip know that you're willing to offer free refreshments or meals to the visiting journalists and travel agents. If you are selected, make sure time is allotted for a guided tour of your store, led by your most knowledgeable manager or salesperson. Present each guest with a press kit. Also, mail press kits to the agents after the tour, since most of them prefer to travel light but accumulate tons of literature and souvenirs on their trips. Making a good impression with travel agents and writers gives you a chance for exposure beyond your own community.

When these agents and writers do visit, make sure that your establishment is in tip-top shape. Your visitors will probably be visiting numerous other hospitality and food establishments, and you want to stand out in every positive way. Only the most memorable businesses will be on their "recommend" list, and you want to be one of them.

Charity for PR

As a good citizen, supporting your local charities is probably something you already do. As a businessperson, you can also use these to enhance your image within the community—a win/win situation for sure. Marketers know that purchasing decisions are based upon emotions. By putting a human face on your business, you'll create a positive image within your community.

There are numerous non-profit organizations that you might consider supporting. Your first concern should be selecting a worthy charity. Look for a charity that is well regarded within the community, fiscally wise and worthy of your time and money. The secondary aspect is the PR value of the support. Look for charities that give you a chance to "show off" your expertise, food specialties and products first. Not only will you be helping to raise money, you'll also be introducing your retail store to the event attendees. There is nothing wrong with clarifying how your support will be recognized and providing the charity with appropriate logos in your press kit. Fundraising experts will understand and won't make you feel like you are "buying" advertising.

A wonderful aspect of charity PR is that you can have a lot of fun. Coach the Little League team you sponsor. Operate the fundraising booth. Serve up a slice of pie. You'll get out of the store and discover the benefits of helping others go well beyond public relations!

Special Events

Special events can be very effective in generating publicity and community interest. You may be opening a new property or celebrating a renovation or an anniversary. Any such occasions are opportunities to plan a special event that will support or improve your PR program. There are usually two kinds of special events: one-time and ongoing. Obviously, you're not going to have a groundbreaking ceremony annually, but you might have a famous Fourth of July party every year.

The key question to ask when designing a special event is "Why?" Clearly defining your objectives before you start is crucial. Is your goal to improve community opinion of your business? To present yourself as a good employer? To show off a renovation?

If you are planning an anniversary celebration, research what events were going on in your community when you opened: Was there a huge fire? Did the President speak at the local college? Once you have this information, send it to the press. They will see your event as part of the historical landscape, as opposed to a commercial endeavor that benefits only you, and they'll appreciate your community focus.

Special events require preparation to ensure everything is ready when the spotlight of attention is aimed at you. Be certain the day you have chosen does not conflict with another potentially competing event or fall on an inappropriate holiday. With a groundbreaking or opening of a new property, you should invite the developer, architect, interior designer, civic officials—all the pertinent folks—and the media. You should prepare brief remarks and ask the architect to comment on the building. In your remarks, remind your listeners that the addition of your business does not boost school taxes or increase the need for police and fire protection; it adds new jobs and new tax revenues.

If you are celebrating an opening, tours of the store are a must and should be led by your most personable employees. Refreshments should be served and plenty of food samples available. Whatever your occasion, you should provide press kits to the attending media and mail them to all media that were invited. Souvenirs are a good idea; they can be simple or elaborate, but should always be creative, fun and useful to your customers.

Talking to Your Community

Your store's success depends upon your community. Retail stores that are not accepted by their local communities disappear. It's as simple as that. In addition, you won't find a prosperous store in a depressed area. Your store can't be successful unless the local community accepts it.

What does that mean to your store? It doesn't simply mean that you should help support good causes. It means your business needs to be a leader in its community. In practice, this means building bridges between your company and your community to maintain and foster your environment in a way that benefits both you and the community. Basically, your goal is to make your immediate world a better place in which everybody can thrive.

The following are a few ideas that can be part of an effective community relations program:

- Fill a community need—create something that wasn't there before.
- Remove something that causes a community problem.
- Include "have-nots" in something that usually excludes them.
- Share your space, equipment or expertise.
- Offer tutoring, or otherwise mobilize your workforce as a helping hand.
- Promote your community elsewhere.

Being a good citizen is, of course, crucial, but you also need to convince your community of the value of your business as a business. Most businesses provide jobs and pay taxes in their communities. Your store can become a community hub. A lecture area or classroom can become a meeting place and a center for important social/economic functions. Decisions that affect the future of your local economy can happen over a pastry and cup of coffee in your store.

These are real benefits, and they should be integrated into the message you send by being a good citizen. Designing this message is a straightforward but remarkably effective process:

- List the things your establishment brings to the community: jobs, taxes, well-maintained architecture, etc.
- List what your business receives from its community: employees, fire and police protection, trash removal, utilities, etc.
- List your business's complaints about your community: high taxes, air pollution, noise pollution, narrow roads, etc.

Once you have outlined these items, look for ways your business can lead the way in improving what doesn't work. As you do this, consult with your local chamber of commerce or visitors' bureau. They may be able to integrate you into existing community betterment programs aimed at your objectives.

If done well, your community relations program will create positive opinions in your community. In turn, this will cause local residents to recommend you to their friends; will encourage people to apply for jobs; and may encourage suppliers to seek to do business with you. In addition, if there is an emergency at your establishment, having a positive standing in the community will enable your employees and business to be treated fairly.

An effective community relations program is a win-win situation because it gives you the opportunity to be a deep and abiding member of your community—improving the quality of life and opportunities around you—and, at the same time, contributes significantly to your bottom line.

Employee Relations Is Also Public Relations

One of the most important "publics" that your public relations program should focus on is your staff. Happy and productive employees are vital to good customer service and they share their feelings outside of work—that's good PR all the way around!

Customers want to be taken care of, and they judge a business as much on the quality of the service as the product. Basically, if a member of your staff is grumpy or tired, that's bad PR. Therefore, employee relations should be a main focus of your PR campaign. In order to do this you must have well-trained staff that understands the technical ins and outs of their jobs and believe in your organization's mission. Your employees need to know the high level of service your customers expect and they need to be empowered to deliver it. A staff that does this on an ongoing basis is one that generates repeat business through word-of-mouth referrals. In addition, that's good PR.

Keeping your employees informed is a key way of making them feel involved and building positive feelings between staff and management. The following is a list of things to communicate to your staff:

- How your business is doing and what you're planning.
- How the competition is doing and what they're planning.
- What community issues you're concerned about and taking a role in.
- Recent and future personnel changes.
- Available training and job openings.

- Staff weddings, birthdays, accomplishments or happenings.
- Ask, listen and act. Don't just tell them; show them how important they are to your business.

Communicating this information gives employees the sense that you care and creates a unified work atmosphere where great service becomes a group responsibility. It also shows that you recognize the difference they make to your bottom line and that you're paying attention.

Opening the lines of communication between management and staff is the next step. No one knows the intimate ins and outs of your business like your staff. If they care about your business and know your ears are open, they can be your biggest resource in suggesting improvements and letting you know what's really going on. One-on-one meetings with supervisors, group meetings, employee newsletters, orientation/review sessions and training meetings are all effective ways to open the channels of communication between you and your employees. These sessions let them know you care and encourage them make the biggest difference they can.

An ongoing employee appreciation program is a good idea. Create a structure that is a part of your daily operation: a large bulletin board in a high-traffic area or a monthly party where awards and prizes are given (cash, great parking spaces, etc.). Give employees something to wear (e.g., a recognition pin) that signifies acknowledgement of the services they provide. Be creative, and find something that effectively and continuously supports the goals of both your employee relations program and your overall PR plan.

Planning for the Unforeseen

When you are knee-deep in an emergency is not the time to develop a crisis plan; you must prepare now. If you have a strategy developed in advance, then when something bad does happen, you assure the most accurate, objective media coverage of the event. It's important that all your employees are aware of this plan and that they are reminded of it regularly. Since your employees generate a huge amount of your PR, it's crucial for them to know how to act and what to say—and not say—during a crisis.

When an employee or guest is injured in your establishment or other negative event occurs, the public often assumes you're guilty whether or not you're even mildly at fault. Therefore, how you handle public relations during this time means the difference between a temporary loss of public support or the permanent loss of a great deal of your business.

Having built strong media relations pays off during an emergency. The person who will be the media liaison during an emergency should be building and nurturing good media relations now, in case anything does happen. With proper PR, you can shift the public from viewing you as incompetent to having more faith than ever in your establishment. Public opinion depends on how effectively you manage information and how well you tell your story.

Your job is to select items that your customers need and want; that you can buy or make at an appropriate price and that you can be profitable selling.

11

Choosing Your Sales Mix

Your gourmet specialty store may be a retail-only store, have wholesale accounts, feature a deli or candy shop, be located in or near a tourist attraction or be a combination of any of these. The products and services you sell are your sales mix. Your job is to select items that your customers need and want; that you can buy or make at an appropriate price and that you can be profitable selling. In this chapter, we'll divide the topic into food, beverage, non-food products and services, and discuss some of the choices you might offer customers.

Food

There are literally thousands of gourmet food choices for you to stock—everything from handmade chocolate truffles to imported caviar. As Americans continue to expand their food interests, most food categories that have grown at unprecedented rates in the last 25 years. In general, virtually everything you might offer can now be found (albeit in a mass-market version) at the grocery store. This covers:

- Cooking and baking ingredients

- Herbs and spices
- Decorative edibles
- Sweet or savory ready-to-eat fare
- Gourmet foods

When choosing food items, you'll need to research the touchstones that attract gourmands to an item.

Quality can be difficult to define. However, your discriminating customers will know it when they see it. Here are how they assess food quality:

- **Looks.** Gourmet food should be visually attractive, from packaging to how it looks on the plate.

- **Smell.** As the cliché goes, "the nose knows." Fragrant and pleasant scents are quality signals. Strong, strange or stale scents put people off.

- **Taste.** You'll want to appeal to educated palates and meet the expectations of discriminating customers.

- **Texture.** Smooth and creamy, soft and velvety, salty and sweet are also ways the tongue identifies quality.

- **Exclusivity.** Rare or not typically found in your community. These can be custom-order items or stocked specialties.

- **Uniqueness.** A regional specialty, ethnic favorite or seasonal food item.

- **Versatility.** Perfect for entertaining and to enhance special meals.

- **Popularity.** Food has its own style and, like all styles, they change with the season and throughout the years. Health concerns, safety issues, economic conditions, weather effects and trends directly affect what we eat.

Making Choices

How do you know what your customers will want? In researching your market, dreaming up your ideal customer and writing your business plan, you should have discovered some needs that you can fill. When talking food, wants become needs; these needs can be physical (fuel and physical satisfaction), emotional (comforting), psychological (rewarding), religious (kosher), health (allergy-free), political (vegetarian) and social (delight your guests). Food is filled with emotional memories and symbolism—it goes well beyond our need to fuel our bodies. As a gourmet specialty business, you'll be stimulating these emotional touchstones. The better you are at finding these and promoting them, the more likely you will be successful.

Emotional Touchstones

Like trends discussed below, emotional touchstones are part of what makes something popular. However, trends tend to evolve based on outside influences while touchstones come more from internalized experiences. Examples of touchstones are Christmas cookies like your mom made, original Coke®, Moon Pies® and comfort foods like macaroni and cheese.

Food Trends

Julia Child's first PBS cooking show ushered in an interest in gourmet food. Intimidating French cuisine suddenly became approachable. Graham Kerr delighted us with his cooking and humorous take on food. Soon, great numbers of immigrants moving into our communities began to share their native dishes. On television, Food TV now offers dozens of programs exploring cooking, food finds, food trends and commercial-grade cooking equipment for the home.

Keeping in touch with what's in and what's out will help you add new items without over-investing in your customers' fleeting interests. The trends discussed here will already have passed from favor when you read this book—that's the way trends work. Imagine the types of foods served at home in the 1950s—green Jell-O® salads, mushroom soup-based casseroles and iceberg wedge salads. While these dishes may still be eaten, they are no longer considered popular. However, trends do tend to be recycled as generations age and become more nostalgic about the "good old days."

"Lasting" Trends

Safety, health, indulgence and convenience are all active trends in food. You'll find your customers are interested in one of these—and sometimes all four—even if they are contradictory! The key to tapping into food trends is to tell them about it. Tell your customers all about your ingredients and how they are good for them (physically and emotionally), how luxurious your food is and how easy it is buy and use. Include descriptive copy and plenty of adjectives!

The following trend categories have affected our food choices for the last decade or more.

Safety

Allergen-free, kosher, chemical-free, natural ingredients, organically grown.

Unlike "health" below, safety goes beyond the personal well-being of your customers and includes a desire to protect the earth by using products grown and produced without harming the planet.

Allergy issues are less affected by trends. By learning about your customers, you can provide special allergen-free products (no eggs, dairy-free, no nuts, etc.). Vegetarian products and kosher foods bridge multiple categories for consumers who are accustomed to paying extra for peace of mind.

Health

Vitamin-rich, natural in nutrients and fiber, filled with antioxidants, prevents disease or illness.

Healthy food choices may be based upon scientific evidence or the latest diet fad. Read the Health section of your local paper to keep in touch with health-related food trends. As a small business, you have the flexibility to take advantages of health-related trends as they come and go.

Indulgence

Rich, creamy, buttery, laden with expensive ingredients.

You'll have customers who will only buy the most indulgent of desserts, and you'll have others who will only splurge for special occasions. You'll even have those who want healthy offerings Monday through Friday, and the diet-busters during the weekend. You'll have customers who buy low-fat milk to go with chocolate cake! Food has "value," and many of your customers feel that they deserve to reward themselves with food favorites.

Convenience

Ready-to-heat packaging, pre-cut, enhancements.

Busy lives mean less time to prepare meals. Prepared foods can be transformed from an ordinary meal into extraordinary with the help of peasant bread, imported cheeses, wine, nice linens or beautiful stemware. Many of your customers enjoy entertaining but busy schedules mean they are looking for convenience without forsaking elegance, taste and fun! Meal enhancements, along with timesaving devices such as pressure cookers and countertop convection ovens, can solve their time problems.

Going Natural

The words "whole wheat," "natural" and "organic" have been tossed around for years in food manufacturers' packaging and marketing. Although the U.S. Food and Drug Administration passed National Organic Program (NOP) Standards (information at www.ams.usda.gov/nop), most "healthy" terms have no federal definition. However, you should do your best to fairly and accurately represent the products you sell in your newsletters, display signs and advertising.

- To learn more about organic foods, find retail/manufacturer training materials and order promotional aids for organic products, visit the Organic Alliance (www.organic.org).

- For information on retail compliance of the NOP, visit this USDA

Web page at www.ams.usda.gov/nop/ProdHandlers/RetailFood-Establishments.html.

- You'll find a helpful consumer's guide at Eco-Labels (www.eco-labels.org).

Local Foods

Fresh means buying locally. The slow food movement also encourages purchasing food with minimal handling from field to consumer. Contact local ranchers and produce growers to develop a program where you promote their products in your store and at farmers' markets. Contact your local health department for food-handling and safety requirements and training.

Your Niche

A gourmet retail shop by definition serves a niche market—those with greater disposable income and an interest in gourmet food. However, within that niche are other smaller niches that you might market to also. This can be done by focusing on a single food or food-related category. By concentrating on a specialty product or two, you'll develop a reputation and fill an underserved market. Look carefully at your competition—examine what they are offering and what they aren't. Look for "weak" spots in their quality, presentation and selection.

You must thoroughly research your potential market to determine if your concept can be profitable. Create break-even scenarios based upon your costs and overhead before you commit a large storefront to a small niche.

Other ways to reach niche markets can be successful by reducing your overhead. Below are a few examples.

- Develop a "store-within-a-store." By subletting space within an existing store, you'll lower your overhead while sharing customer bases.

- Create in-store profit centers, where displays and marketing focus on your niche without abandoning a broader product selection. Keep separate accounting and sales records to access profitability of these profit centers.

- Kiosks and common area displays in malls can be a way to promote niche products. This is another concept where you receive benefits from the mall's marketing and surrounding stores. Foot traffic analysis should be done to determine whether your mall and/or location within the mall attract enough interested customers.

Sweets

Feed their sweet tooth to feed your bottom line. A variety of dessert items can be added to your product mix that can be sold whole (like tarts or cheesecakes) or sold in individual servings (mousse cakes or cobblers). Individual servings are becoming extremely popular as the number of single diners continues to increase across the United States. Review your customer demographics to see what demographic trends are happening in your neighborhood.

- Take a single item, like ice cream, and build a display filled with rich toppings, fun bowls, practical scoops, ice cream makers and cookbooks.

- Determine storage and refrigeration requirements and their related costs before committing to perishable products.

- Consider offering mouth-watering candies, nuts or other impulse food items. Your choices should appeal to your customers, take into account your foot traffic and potential tourist appeal.

Beverages

What finishes a good meal, tingles the taste buds, clears the palate, enhances tastes, refreshes you, relaxes or stimulates you? A beverage, of course.

Coffee

- Plain, decaf, iced or hot coffee-based drinks.
- Whole or fresh-ground coffee beans for home or office brewing.
- Glasses or cups ready-to-drink.
- Coffee enhancements, such as liquid or "spice" flavorings.
- Brewing, grinding and serving equipment and tools.

Tea

- Iced or hot.
- Loose leaves or bagged teas from around the world.
- Black, green, herbal, flavored, concentrates or Chai variations.
- Glasses and cups ready-to drink.
- Tea pots, strainers, cups and ice tea machines.
- Tea enhancements, such as sugars and lemon drops.

Juices

- Unique blends to drink straight or use as mixers.

Mixers and Flavor Enhancers

- Prepared cocktail mixers for margaritas, piña coladas or coffee nudges.
- Italian syrups and flavorings.

Trendy Drinks

- Juice-based, tea-based, herbal, energy drinks.

Soda

- Imported or ethnic brands.

Coffee

If you are going to serve coffee drinks, you could buy all your own roasting, grinding and brewing equipment and pay to have someone install and maintain it. This would enable you to purchase coffee from any company at reduced prices. However, a large capital outlay would be necessary. Since there is no great advantage to doing this, it is recommended that you use the coffee distributor contract method.

There are many different coffee blends available. Invest in the finest and most popular blends available. Select at least one of each: dark roast, medium body, light blend and decaf. There are literally dozens of popular flavored coffees (such as hazelnut, vanilla and chocolate-mint) that you can offer. Try the different blends under consideration in a blind taste test.

Specialty Coffee Machines

Coffee is no longer a simple mug of decaf or regular Joe. The growth of specialty coffee drinks means your customers will be asking for a grande vanilla latte or a raspberry mocha. Espresso machines can run into the thousands of dollars and require a skilled barista to operate. Your coffee vendor can help you assess your needs based upon customer demographics, volume and budget. Espresso systems can be expensive to operate and maintain so explore your options before signing a contract.

For more information on espresso machines, visit Espresso Business at www.espressobusiness.com and Whole Latte Love at www.wholelattelove.com.

Complementary Products

If your retail offerings are primarily food, you may want to carry a few complementary goods that enhance the food items or are commonly used in preparing, storing or serving these. And don't forget cookbooks! A single recipe can spur a customer to purchase a few jars of spices and invest in a new KitchenAid® mixer along with the meat grinder attachment and a book on sausage-making.

The most obvious choices for non-food items would be goods that enhance your customers' use of your retail food items. The following pages has a few examples to get you thinking about the possibilities.

COMPLEMENTARY PRODUCTS	
If You Sell...	**Complementary Product**
Coffee	Insulated coffee mugs
Tea leaves	Tea strainers
Spices	Salt & pepper mills
Olive oil	Decorative serving sets
Fresh herbs	Water-filled storage containers
Jams and jellies	Serving bowls
Olives	Olive forks
Whole nuts	Nut crackers
Bread flour	Bread-making cookbooks

Offering complementary products isn't just a way to sell something else—it gives people ideas and reasons to purchase your primary products.

Selling Food Prep, Serving and Storage Products

A gourmet specialty shop may, in fact, never sell any food. Just as food choices abound, so do the international selection of food-related products. Generally you can divide these into products that are used in preparing food, products that are used in serving food and products that are used in storing food. Just as our food choices have become so vast, so have our choices in equipment, tools and accessories. Food equipment typically refers to larger ticket items such as ovens, toasters and cookware. Food tools are things like whisks, knives and cheese cutters. Food accessories are things like cupcake papers, serving bowls and carafes.

The premiere trade show for cooking equipment, the annual International Housewares Show in Chicago is where all the latest and greatest equipment and tools are introduced to the world. Trends for the upcoming season and beyond, along with the newest versions of popular brands, are all there for you to learn about and see.

Food Equipment

The equipment you actually need to prepare a meal is very basic. You need a heat source, a pot or bowl to cook in, something to stir or turn the food and a utensil to eat with (fingers are a utensil here). In fact, you might only need your fingers if you eat the food raw. But our preferred foods have evolved significantly since the days when a bowl of gruel and a few nuts were considered a meal.

As our food choices have become more sophisticated and influenced by other cultures, our choices in food equipment have also become more sophisticated. Some equipment can be used every day in a variety of ways with a variety of foods. Others are "specialty" items used once a year for a holiday treat, occasionally for special meals or are only used for a single purpose.

Food equipment choices are also affected by trends. You'll find a few trend categories and examples below. As food trends evolve, so do the products used to prepare them.

- **Style and color.** Color-matched blenders, mixers and toasters.
- **Materials.** Stainless steel, space-age plastics and others.
- **Cooking method.** Pressure cookers, slow-cookers, fondue pots and grills.
- **Power source.** Electric tea kettles, electric pressure cookers and grills.

Style and Color

High-end kitchen equipment can be divided into two categories in regards to appearance:

- **Industrial/professional.** Function over appearance—for those wanting to look like a pro.

- **Artistic.** Appearance first, function second—stylish colors such as in the KitchenAid® line are common, while art deco influences are starting to be seen in toasters and blenders. The retro look continues in lines and material choices.

Keep in touch with the up and coming colors and create a "color explosion display" featuring equipment, tools, serving ware and linens that coordinate.

Professional Equipment

Professional-grade equipment, including brand names previously only available through restaurant supply stores, has become highly desirable. Although there is no established performance or quality standards for the terms "professional-grade" or "commercial-grade," consumers make assumptions about the superiority of products labeled as such.

Along with commercial brands, professionals such as Wolfgang Puck offer private label products, such as knives and cookware, marketed under their name. Other well-known chefs endorse consumer product lines. This name recognition adds value and credence to your message of superiority and performance. Don't forget to take advantage of this recognition with manufacturer-provided sales and promotional materials for your advertising and in-store displays.

Specialty Equipment

Specialty equipment, such as a raclette or Panini sandwich grills, have limited appeal in smaller markets. It is important that these are researched well before committing shelf space. Ethnic cuisine can rely on unfamiliar equipment so learn more about local favorites or ways to introduce new items. Promoting the equipment along with mini-classes, free recipes and eye-level displays can keep these in demand.

Specialty equipment sales are directly related to food trends. Remember when fondue pots where all the rage? They have cycled in and out (although never like during their 1970s peak). Keep tabs on those "everything old is new again" products.

Cooks Love Gadgets

If cooking is a passion, it is difficult to resist the thousands of cooking and serving tools and gadgets available. Everything you can imagine is available—from an apple peeler to an escargot fork to a tuna can strainer. So how do you choose? First, start with the basics, then add gourmet choices, ethnic needs and the merely whimsical.

The Basics

If you have been cooking for years, you might not think about what every kitchen should own (in fact, you may actually own multiple versions of each!). The Reluctant Gourmet Web site at www.reluctantgourmet.com details new kitchen/beginner cook's needs. A more comprehensive guide is *The Kitchenware Book* by Irena Chalmers and Steve Ettlinger.

The typical items such as measuring cups (liquid and dry) and spoons, knives, peelers, can openers, spatulas, timers and basic bakeware will be on everyone's lists. Create a master list and select the most practical and quality versions you can locate.

You might offer free classes called "Outfitting Your Kitchen" or "Tools to Get You Started" to share the passion and create new customers!

Beyond the Basics

The tools and gadgets "beyond the basics" tend to be:

- Impulse buys for people who enjoy owning the latest and greatest. Select products and create displays to catch their eye.
- Used by people expanding their culinary skills. Cross-market books, free recipes and offer classes to create a demand for specific products.

- Those who need more specialized tools to save time or enhance quality. Organize tools and gadgets by function so people looking for a measuring cup will find the one that works great with sticky ingredients.

- Recipe-specific recommendations where substitutions aren't familiar.
  - You cannot anticipate what recipes will bring people into your store; however, you can work closely with your newspaper's food editor to let people know that you carry items mentioned in upcoming articles.
  - Review the major culinary publications as they hit the newsstand to be prepared for requests.
  - Advertise that you carry what they are seeking (i.e., As seen in the March issue of Gourmet…").

In *Cooking Essentials for the New Professional Chef* by The Food and Beverage Institute and Mary Deirdre Donovan, you'll find plenty of ideas for your more skilled customers.

Your Own Products

Perhaps your interest in starting a specialty food retail store is based on your desire to market your own food products. Just like Paul Newman's homemade salad dressing, Aunt Betty's famous eggnog or your mouthwatering cheesecake can be the catalyst for a great business. We won't discuss the manufacturing process for creating consumer food products here; however, we will address ways to use your own products as a foundation and/or focal point of your store.

Your products' logo, labels and advertising should integrate with your store image, logo and tagline. However, it will need a distinct look and advertising campaign. You don't want people to think that is all you carry in your store.

In-store displays of your featured product(s) should be created to catch the eye and then move the shopper to look for complementary or companion products. Think of your product and look for other items that would encourage people to try them. Don't just sell an unfamiliar product—give them ideas and ways to use it!

- **Make jam?** Offer toasters, bread knives, butter servers, serving spoons and jars.
- **Make cocktail mixers?** Stock shakers, rimmers, bartender guides, blenders and glasses.
- **Make catsup?** Include other gourmet condiments such as chutneys, mustards, salsas and flavored mayonnaises.

Shopping

Selecting your resale products will require some research and aggressive shopping. Below are some resources and tips for locating the best products for your customers.

- **Gift marts.** Although you might not sell what one might think of as "gift items," thousands of food and food-related products from cookbooks to martini glasses are marketed by manufacturers through sales rep groups that operate out of wholesale markets known as gift marts. On the Internet, use the keywords "gift mart" to locate the one nearest your town.
- **Wholesalers/Distributors.** Yahoo and Google have directories where food and food-related wholesalers are listed. Check these to locate national and regional sources. Your local restaurant supply house can also be of assistance. Other directories online can be found at www.foodcontact.com.
- **Trade publications.** Subscribe to publications such as Gourmet Retailing and Gourmet News.
- **Trade shows.** Walk the various trade shows. Manufacturer rep groups can provide you with the dates and information on regional and international food and houseware shows of interest. To follow are a few shows of interest. (Additional organization and trade show

information can be found in Chapter 23.)

- Show listings can be found at Produx.com—www.produx.com
- The Gourmet Products Show—www.thegourmetshow.com
- Fancy Food Show—www.specialtyfood.com
- National Hardware Show—www.nationalhardwareshow.com
- Canadian International Food & Beverage Show—www.crfa.ca
- National Fiery Foods Show—www.fiery-foods.com
- Gourmet Shows—www.gourmetshows.com
- International Home & Housewares Show—www.housewares.org
- Coffee Fest—www.coffeefest.com

12

Equipping Your Store

Your equipment, fixtures and tools are an investment in your ability to offer the products and services your customers want quickly and efficiently. Equipment has an ROI factor that makes it pay for itself over time. The shorter the repayment time, the better investment for your business. The ROI can be calculated in dollars (increased sales, fewer employees) and time (faster production). Other important benefits are often difficult to put into comparable numbers, such as improved quality (happier customers), reduced risk (reduced injuries and stress) and competitive advantage (exclusivity, enhanced service, more choices).

When we refer to equipment for your store in this chapter, we are including sales tools (cash registers), accounting tools (inventory scanners), fixtures (storage and display, walls, freestanding and point-of-sale) and facility equipment (vacuums and intercoms).

Equipment Budgeting

The #1 question is "How much should I spend?" Quality and pricing levels vary widely so there is no easy answer. We do know that successful retailers won't spend more than they need to.

For some light-duty equipment, a less expensive, yet highly serviceable brand may be the best choice, while heavy-use equipment may require the best quality available for lasting performance.

How Do I Keep Within My Budget?

First, develop an equipment/fixture/tool wish list. Divide your list into three priority categories: Cannot Live Without, Would Make Life Easier and Wouldn't It Be Great?

- Allocate your budget primarily to the first category. This is the equipment that makes you money.
- Review the items in category two for potential time and money-savings.
- Be very objective about items in category three. Will the $14,000 espresso machine make a difference in your bottom line?
- Analyze your second and third category items for their potential ROI. How long it will take to pay for itself? Will it make you money or just make you look better? Is leasing a wise alternative?
- Review every decision from your CPA's viewpoint. Buying equipment can be like getting a new toy; don't let your excitement or a salesperson's pitch eat up your budget.
- Ask about last years' models. Incentives may be available on older or overstocked models.
- Check the Internet for discounts. Search for "retail [equipment name]." Often equipment is drop-shipped from the factory, so freight may not be a factor. Ask about sales tax, as this is a "gray" area for online purchases.

Buying Used Equipment

Buying used retail equipment and fixtures can be a very wise decision. Just like a used car, equipment depreciates more during the first year or two. When examining used equipment, you'll need to assess its functionality (will it work for me?) and its appearance (does it look new?).

- Before searching for a used piece of equipment, shop for new. This will give you a benchmark of features, quality levels among manufacturers and pricing. Just as a used Mercedes is a safer investment than a used Yugo, focus on the top manufacturers with a reputation for quality.

- Ask about the repair history of the make/model. Commercial equipment typically has a longer projected lifespan. Your dealer will probably have personal experience with the equipment.

- Learn the term "reconditioned." Reconditioned equipment has been cleaned, worn/broken parts replaced and a short dealer warranty. Typically priced 40 to 50 percent of new.

- Learn the term "rebuilt." Rebuilt equipment has been totally dismantled and rebuilt, longer dealer warranty. Should perform equal to the manufacturer's specs. Typically priced 50 to 70 percent of new.

- Verify the equipment's age and history. Use manufacturer serial numbers and service records to check age and care. Don't rely on an "only driven on Sundays by Grandma" story.

- Ask the used equipment supplier about their trade-in policy. Some suppliers will give you above-average trade-in values when returning to purchase a new version.

- Shop for used equipment online (auction and direct purchase sites), at bankruptcy auctions, from new equipment dealers and manufacturers' rep groups.

- Ask if they have demo models available. Trade show, showroom and test models typically have few "miles" on them and reduced "scratch 'n dent" prices.

- Save time by buying used. Lead times on new equipment can be lengthy.

Don't Buy:

- Cosmetically damaged equipment/fixtures that will be visible to customers.
- Anything with moderate (or worse) rust (except restorable cast iron).
- "Married" equipment (where the legs from one model have been attached erroneously to another model).
- Foreign-made equipment that wasn't made specifically for the U.S. market. Unknown electrical conversions can be a problem.

Leasing Your Equipment

For some storeowners, leasing can be a way to extend your available capital. Leasing is 100 percent financing. Depending on your lease, you may receive better tax benefits at lower monthly payments while preserving your working capital and borrowing capabilities. To help you determine what financing method suits your needs, here are some helpful ideas and resources:

- **Don't think of leasing as easy money.** The true cost of leased equipment can be much greater than the purchase price. You are paying interest even when you lease.
- **Avoid personal guarantees if possible.** If you sign it, you're liable even if your store closes or the equipment doesn't last.
- **Educate yourself about leasing** before shopping for a leasing company. Leasing companies pull credit reports. Too many inquiries can negatively affect your credit reputation.
- **Confirm who is responsible for service and maintenance.** The

manufacturer's warranty is usually extended to the lessee. However, in most cases, you are 100 percent responsible for keeping the equipment in good working order and resalable condition.

- **Compare your total annual lease costs to your annual depreciation benefits.** Most equipment has a 7-year depreciation rate; typical leases are 36 to 60 months.
- **Don't lease items with a short life** or items that are fully deductible the purchase year.
- **Be aware of leases with low buy-out provisions.** The IRS may classify it as a purchase agreement subject to depreciation rules instead of a 100 percent expense.
- **Make certain your insurance adequately covers leased equipment** for fire, theft or other losses.
- **Get the fair market value information in writing.** Equipment with unrealistic residual values can have excessive buyouts. Check the used market for comparison figures.
- **Read the lease before signing.** A lease is a legal contract. You might even want to have your lawyer review the fine print.
- **Estimate your monthly payments** and learn more about leasing from GE Leasing Solutions at www.geleasingsolutions.com.
- **Ask about used equipment leasing.** This can be a cost-effective way to obtain the most expensive equipment.

Making Wise Equipment Purchases

Your job in choosing equipment is to get the best value for every dollar spent. We've outlined some helpful suggestions to ensure that you get the quality, service and performance you pay for and need.

- **Seek out recommendations.** Unfortunately, there is no *Consumer*

Reports for retail and commercial equipment. But asking peers, used equipment dealers, industry association members and equipment specialists can help you learn about desired features, life expectancies and brand names to consider and/or avoid.

- **Comparison shop.** Have your consultant or equipment dealer give you good/better/best recommendations. Compare features, operation costs and life expectancies.

- **Establish substitution rules.** Sometimes the equipment you select is not available due to excessive lead times, product discontinuation or unforeseen price increases. Carefully examine substitutions.

- **Don't have equipment delivered until you are ready to install it;** you risk dents and dings. Dust can irreparably damage some fragile equipment.

Which Quality Level?

Should I invest in the top brand on the market, or purchase a serviceable low-end model? Who wouldn't want the latest and greatest of retail, office and business equipment? Investing wisely is a contributing factor in your long-term success.

We suggest that you carefully weigh your emotional, creative and business needs in assessing whether a specific piece of equipment, tool or fixture serves your immediate and future needs. Ask the following decision-making questions:

- Does it meet my budget?
- Does smaller, more efficient equipment save precious space?
- Will my service quality improve with this equipment?
- What is the return on investment?
- For specialty equipment, will I sell enough to pay for it?
- Will it be on display where looks are important?
- What type of routine maintenance does it require?
- Is local service available and affordable?

- Is it difficult or expensive to operate daily?
- Is an economical service and/or maintenance contract available?
- Is it the most productive and energy-efficient equipment for the job?
- Is the lifespan greater than the payment or lease terms?
- Are there trade-in/trade-up programs available?
- What's the resale value if I need to sell or trade-up?
- Does it meet sanitation, plumbing or building code requirements?
- Will it save energy costs, reduce overhead or make employees more productive?

Service Contracts

Many equipment manufacturers have service contracts that may be purchased. If available, it is highly recommended that you purchase them. Equipment that is maintained to the manufacturer's specifications will last longer and operate more effectively and efficiently.

Equipment Records

Set up a loose-leaf binder to contain all the information on your equipment and its maintenance schedules. Included in this binder should be warranties, brochures, equipment schematics, operating instructions, maintenance schedules, part lists, order forms, past service records, manufacturers' phone numbers, a chart showing which circuit breaker operates each piece of equipment, etc. Keep this manual up to date from the very beginning. Become aware of your equipments' needs and act accordingly. Train your employees in the proper use of your equipment and it will serve the store well for many years.

Retail-Specific Equipment, Tools and Supplies

Displays and Fixtures

Displays and fixtures are more than storage units—they are merchandising tools that properly show off your wares and help customers make selections. When purchasing displays and fixtures, you are buying for today and the future, so look for versatility. Can shelves be easily adjusted? Can longer pegs be used? Can they be repainted? Are additional customizing components available?

To properly store and merchandise your product offerings, you need to select the best display cases and fixtures for the job. Displays can be:

- **Functional**—traditional sliding or swinging glass doors.
- **Elegant** –European-style wood racks.
- **Temporary**—freestanding cardboard displays.
- **Classic**—old-fashioned tubs with ice holding bottles of water.
- **Creative**—combine boxes, shelves, stands, wagons, strollers and décor for innovative displays.

Wall Fixtures

Wall fixtures can be permanently mounted to the wall such as wire grid systems, slatwall or pegboard styles or can be freestanding units designed to line your store walls. The first thing you need to consider when reviewing potential fixture choices is stability, strength and weight loads. A top-heavy unit or wobbly shelf is a disaster waiting to happen.

Freestanding Fixtures

Freestanding simply refers to that fact that these displays do not require additional support. Aisle shelving, cardboard point-of-sale bins, revolving showcases and furniture-style table displays are all freestanding.

Retail displays aren't your only choices. You can use a variety of items and materials to create a unique display cabinet, shelf or table. Antique kitchen stoves, a 50s dinette set or an elegant dining table are all possibilities. Check out local thrift and antique stores for items that can be recycled into a custom display.

Showcases

Showcases (also known as display cases) can be horizontal or vertical glass displays capable of holding fragile goods, expensive products or refrigerated items. Knowing your product mix and front-of-the-store layout will help you decide on the best cases for your needs.

Having ample displays is critical so carefully chart out your retail area to maximize the space with under-counter displays, wall-sized displays, freestanding vertical merchandisers and movable units for temporary promotions. When laying the room out, think about how your ideal customer will enter and approach each display. Will they sweep the room looking for just the right loaf of bread or cake? Will they walk directly up to the counter to order?

When choosing a display, think about how a grocery store merchandises cereal: the most expensive "adult" products are at the top (within an adult's reach), the desirable high-profit "kids" products are stocked in the middle of the shelves (impulse items for kids) and the lower-profit bulk and generic brands are on the lowest shelves. Determine your low-, average- and high-profit items and display them accordingly. High-traffic items, such as bagels or donuts in the morning and loaves of bread in the afternoon, can be stocked on an eye-level shelf and the "off schedule" items moved to a less prominent position.

Countertop Displays

Eye-level displays on your counter can be quite effective in merchandising new food items or hot enticements like fresh cookies. Just don't overwhelm the active work areas and cash register. People don't like to feel like other people are pressing in around them when they are opening their purse or wallet.

These displays can be temporary cardboard merchandise displays provided by the supplier, attractive chrome and glass units, unique bowls or stands; just about anything that makes it easy for customers to make a last-minute choice just before being rung up.

Refrigerated Displays

When selecting a refrigerated display case, look for easy-to-clean units with removable components and no hard-to-reach areas. Adjustable shelving that can accommodate the tallest cake or multilevel displays is an added benefit.

Also, be sure to purchase an energy-efficient refrigerated mode and compare energy ratings. Avoid older, used showcases your initial savings probably won't offset the extra energy cost. To lower your utility bills:

- Use insulated night covers on display cases.
- Clean condenser coils, fans and gaskets weekly.
- Inspect rubber sealant and gaskets regularly; replace as needed.
- Remove "unnecessary" internal case lights if you have ample ambient light.
- Check and calibrate the thermometer regularly.
- Don't overload refrigerated cases.
- Select the higher energy efficiency rating (EER). The greater the cooling capacity for each kilowatt-hour of energy input, the greater the efficiency of the system.

Package It Up

You'll need a variety of packaging depending upon how your customers purchase and carry specific goods. Some items will do best if packaged in plastic bags; however, you may find that paper products are better accepted by customers who shop at independent retail stores.

Plastic Please

Create custom-imprinted food-safe bags that feature your store logo along with contact information.

Larger "shopping" bags from a durable plastic material and reinforced handle are a good choice for carrying bulky and/or heavy items. Again, these should be decorated with your store logo and tagline (sales pitch line).

Paper Please

Paper bags can have a more "elegant" or "stylish" feel. Whether you want an unbleached, rustic look or a classic white bag, you should match your bag to your store décor/theme/style. A variety of bags and protective packaging should be purchased. Ask your supplier to visit with samples of standard sized bags (using standard sizes is more cost-effective; however, custom bags are also an option). Have product samples available to select the fewest bag configurations that will fit the most products.

Gift boxes (along with free wrapping) can add that special touch to items purchased for giving. This "extra service" can be a great way to build word-of-mouth. Boxes can be:

- White and wrapped with a simple gold ribbon.
- Your store's signature color with coordinating ribbon and instead of a bow, tie on a small whisk or measuring spoon set.
- Wrapped in heavy-duty wrapping paper in elegant and/or colorful fun designs.

Don't forget to include an invitation for the recipient to visit your store. These can be a small, ivory calling card-style with store information or your current newsletter.

Scales

If you sell products that must be weighted (coffee, candy, etc.), invest in accurate scales. Digital scales can be a wise choice as they are faster to read and more accurate, and many display the weight even after removing the bag or bowl. All scales require periodic calibration to ensure accuracy. When investigating a supplier, ask about maintenance and calibration service.

Cash Registers

Most modern cash registers are actually single-purpose computers. Well-known calculator companies, such as Casio, offer a variety of inexpensive units that can provide you with basic recordkeeping and ring up sales quickly. Antique or refurbished cash registers are also an option. However, after reading the next section you may want to consider a computerized model that can provide you with valuable decision-making information.

Computers — How to Use and Profit from Them

Computers have become valuable tools for the small-business owner. They offer capabilities that were once only available to major corporations. Even the smallest retail operation can benefit from owning at least one personal computer. This can be a desktop or laptop model capable of running a word processor, spreadsheet, database, the accounting package of your choice and other off-the-shelf software packages that make your business more organized or efficient.

Computers are integrated into all facets of the retail industry. Computers can:

- Track your sales and purchases.
- Monitor your inventory.
- Increase your purchasing power.
- Maintain accounting records and payroll.
- Provide another way to communicate with customers and employees.

A computer can put your daily accounting in order, print out payroll checks and keep track of customer mailing lists. Even if you outsource these tasks, having a computer to prepare raw data and present it to your consultant is important.

Industry- and task-specific computer systems may not look like a computer—there may not be a monitor and the keyboard may look like a cash register. These specialized systems focus on specific functions such as ringing up sales or calculating weights. Computerized systems, such as with alarm and fire suppression systems, can actually be lifesavers.

Computers are valuable tools for the small-business owner; however, they can also be a source for headaches. It's thorough training that turns all those chips and circuits into a valuable support system. Investing in technology is a poor choice, if you don't likewise invest in learning how to use it. Your local community college, computer store and private learning centers can provide you with fast-track classes with hands-on training for everything from learning Microsoft Windows® to mastering Microsoft Excel® spreadsheets to building your own Web site.

When purchasing custom software or hardware systems, be certain that training is available, manuals are easy to read and on-going support is provided. Industry- and task-specific computerization is a long-term investment. New employees and new business needs require long-term support by your vendor so research these companies before purchasing.

Business Computers

Your personal computer (PC) can be used for accounting, inventory control, personnel support, advertising and business correspondence. Although Apple's Macintosh line has become more popular, we recommend that you invest in a Windows-based system as you'll have access to a greater selection of business and industry-specific software packages. Laptops may be a convenient option; however, your confidential data is at greater risk of being stolen.

Many major computer manufacturers and retailers offer small-business leasing. An extended warranty and/or service agreement (preferably an on-site agreement) can be an excellent investment as your "business" will depend upon your computer working full-time.

For personal computer reviews and recommendations, check publications such as PC World, ZDNet (www.zdnet.com) and C/Net (www.cnet.com). Unless you are running CAD (computer-aided design) or 3-D games, a low- to mid-range small-business system will typically satisfy all your needs.

The World Wide Web

The Web gives small-business owners access to a wealth of information and resources. You can research equipment, place your flour order, compare prices for paper goods and advertise your store with a modem or broadband (high-speed) connection.

Most computer systems include a 56K modem for dial-up service. Be certain to specify this inexpensive add-on if it is not standard. Even if you will be connecting to the Web via DSL (telephone) or cable modem, having dial-up capabilities gives you a back up. Some broadband companies will provide you with limited dial-up access and there are also free dial-up access services available (search the Web for "free dial up").

If you will be maintaining your own Web site or sharing large files with a franchiser, invest in the significantly faster broadband service. Contact your local cable and telephone companies to determine service availability. National companies such as EarthLink and DirecTV also have high-speed access.

Please be aware that always-on connections such as DSL and cable modems mean you have to have extra computer security. Windows XP has a built-in software firewall (to stop electronic intruders from accessing your computer and data), but an additional firewall (software and/or hardware) may be necessary to protect your privacy and confidential files.

A growing number of companies now offer online ordering, order tracking and technical support. The ability to automate repetitive actions can be a real time-saver. If your typical order is stored online, then it takes only a minute to schedule next week's delivery.

Most banks offer Web access to your accounts including transferring funds from one account to another and paying loans and credit cards. Look into Web-based bill paying services through your bank or third-party services such as MyCheckFree (www.mycheckfree.com) and PayTrust (www.paytrust .com) to make billing paying go faster. Individual credit card companies and even utility companies are now offering online bill paying. Check with your creditor for automatic bill paying methods to save you time and keep your account current.

Just be aware of how long it will take for your creditor to actually receive and post the funds. Just because you are paying online doesn't always mean that your bill can be paid on the day it is due; read the fine print carefully! Other bonuses are that you may be able to use a credit card, you get an immediate receipt to print, checks are never lost in the mail and you contact customer service at your convenience.

Computer Networks

Small retail stores probably won't require full networking capabilities, where individual computers can "talk" to each other, share data, printers and Internet access. Networks can be created via existing telephone wiring, data-only wiring or a wireless setup. A local company specializing in networking can advise you of the best solution for your building.

However, if your budget allows and you need greater computing power, a network can become a useful tool to improve your efficiency and control costs.

There are also Web-based ways to access data from remote locations. "Remote" can mean from the front-of-the-house or from your home office. GoToMyPC (www.gotomypc.com) offers Internet-based access. Software programs such as Laplink (www.laplink.com) and pcAnywhere (www .symantec.com/pcanywhere/Consumer) can give you access to your on-site business computer from a home computer or laptop.

Retail-Specific Computer Systems

Point-of-Sale Systems

The most widely used technology in the retail industry is the POS (point-of-sale) system. This system is more than a cash register as it can be programmed to provide a great deal of valuable information. Freestanding and integrated (networked with your accounting system) systems are available in a variety of price ranges; although, all are more expensive than a cash register. Systems can use barcode scanning technology or touch-screen formats. Both are effortless, require minimal training and provide extensive sales data.

Understanding the numbers collected by a POS system gives you more control over your inventory, provides time-specific data (what sells during what hours or days) and provides detailed sales reports.

This information will help you schedule employees to maximize customer service and minimize overtime, monitor shrinkage (waste, theft) and identify productive and non-productive profit centers.

Understanding your POS system ultimately clarifies the bottom line, knocking guesswork out of the equation while paying for itself. Some benefits of using a POS system include:

- Increases sales and accounting information.
- Offers custom tracking and reporting.
- Reports product sales breakdown for forecasting.
- Shows peak and slow periods for better staffing projections.
- Reports individual product performance.
- Monitors inventory usage.
- Processes credit cards immediately.
- Eliminates math errors and minimizes over/under-rings.
- Controls discounting.
- Ends errors caused by poor handwriting.
- Highlights possible theft of money and inventory.
- Records employee timekeeping.
- Tallies employee sales and performance.

General Retail POS Systems

There are literally hundreds of POS systems for general retail use. It can be confusing and an error can be costly. Don't rely on the recommendations of a computer consultant, as they aren't typically experienced number crunchers. Your accountant should be able to provide you with recommendations. Your local retail equipment supplier will also offer POS systems or can provide you with local references.

In selecting a POS system and other accounting software, look for one with convenient training and support and fast local repair service. Research the software company thoroughly—for history of performance and long-term stability—as you'll need them long after the sale!

Choose Your Software First

Find software with the features and reports that best suits your specific business. Then find the right hardware (cash register, computer, printers, etc.) to operate it. Your most versatile choice is software based on Microsoft's Windows operating system (typically Windows 2000 or XP Professional).

However, excellent programs also run on UNIX or Linux operating systems, and you'll need the right hardware/operating system to access these. Custom programmed software that works only with the vendor's hardware means that you are tied to that company even if you are unhappy with their product or service.

The manufacturer's representative can provide you with sample reports and local references. CPA Online has a free research site on locating accounting software at www.findaccountingsoftware.com where you can also research POS systems. Below are just a few general-purpose POS systems for retailers.

- **QuickBooks Point-of-Sale Software (www.intuit.com)** integrates with your QuickBooks for Retailers accounting software and offers a variety of merchant services including credit card processing.
- **Microsoft Business Solutions** (www.microsoft.com/BusinessSolutions) offers a variety of POS and credit card systems along with accounting.
- **The Retail Solution** offers retail POS systems (www.nwns.com).
- **IBM Retail Store Solutions** (www.pc.ibm.com/store/products/pos/sureone) offers a system with a small footprint priced for budget-conscious retailers.

Employee Scheduling and Attendance Software

There are a variety of scheduling and timekeeping software packages along with time-clock based systems to help you schedule and track employee work hours.

Employee Schedule Partner is a complete software package for employee scheduling. Point and click: make a schedule without touching the keyboard. Click a button and the software will fill your schedule with employees automatically. Click a button to replace absent employees, and a list of available employees with phone numbers will appear. The online coach will give helpful hints to new users. Accommodates an unlimited number of employees and positions. You can manually override selections at any time and track employees' availability restrictions. Track payroll and hourly schedule totals for easy budget management. Schedules can begin on any day of the week. Track stations as well as positions. Specify maximum hours per day, days per week and shifts per day for each employee. Lock any employee into a scheduled shift so the program will not move them when juggling the schedule. Save old schedules for reference when needed. The software is even password-protected to prevent unauthorized use. Employee Schedule Partner is available from Atlantic Publishing Company (www.atlantic-pub.com, 800-541-1336).

Employee Time Clock Partner

A hands-down favorite time clock software is Employee Time Clock. This is a complete employee time clock software package. It is very powerful, yet simple to use. Automatically clock in and out (just enter your employee number). Employees can view their time cards to verify information. Password-protected so only management may edit time card information. Even calculates overtime, both daily and weekly. Management can assign Employee ID number or PIN (personal identification number). Employee Time Clock Partner is also available from Atlantic Publishing Company (www.atlantic-pub.com, 800-541-1336).

Accounting Software

Computer programs such as QuickBooks® (www.quickbooks.com) or Peachtree® (www.peachtree.com) are a solid choice for in-house bookkeeping. These programs are inexpensive, easy to use and will save time, money and countless errors. (See Chapter 19 for info on accounting software.)

Other Computer Uses

Since the introduction of desktop computers, small-business owners have leveraged their capabilities to:

- Improve their communications—Web sites, e-mail, blogs.
- Promote their business—brochures, flyers, Web sites.
- Become their own "printer"—business cards, menus, coupons.
- Attract customers—free Internet access.
- Recognize customers—photo displays, bulletin boards.

13

Public Areas of Your Store

First impressions are important to any business, and for a gourmet store they are exceptionally critical. Customers will judge you based upon your public areas—service counters, aisles, walls and restrooms. Your store must be:

- **Attractive**—A visually stimulating place to shop or linger.
- **Clean**—A clean store makes people feel confident that you care.
- **Efficient**—Good service depends upon an efficient workplace.
- **Organized**—A well-organized work area will speed up and enhance your service.
- **Inviting**—A combination of sights, smells and personality that encourages people to return.

From your front door to your restrooms, you can create a great impression by paying attention to details.

Creating a Design Focal Point

What we mean is a design concept that accentuates your products and becomes focal point from which to develop an image (your brand). Here are some creative ideas to help you select and develop your store's design focal point.

- **Choose a design focal point** that reflects your vision, then build upon it. For example, if your focus is imported cheese, incorporate it in your:
    - Store name—Cheese Haven
    - Logo, signs—Beautiful diorama of visually identifiable cheeses such as round Gouda and Swiss.
    - Decorative accents—Strong, contrasting colors to set off neutral color of cheese.

- **Sometimes your design focal point has no point at all.** Design for a feeling using elements makes you think: elegant, cozy, warm, safe, wealthy, rested, young, spoiled.

- **Plan for the future.** Store décor has a 3- to 5-year year lifespan. Concentrate on versatile and neutral foundation elements (floors, lights, ceilings, fixtures) that won't need to be tossed when you redecorate.

- **Spend more on quality basics** and save on the decorative touches. Unlike retail stores where everything is part of the total look, using a design focal point allows you to accessorize without breaking the budget.

- **Don't over-design.** Use blank spaces (bare walls, neutral floors) to ease the eye.

Exterior Areas

Most retail stores don't need outdoor seating or places for customers to linger. However, the area surrounding your store (whether it is in an enclosed mall or outdoors) is considered your "sphere of influence." This sphere may not formally be your responsibility, but you should do your best to keep this area inviting for customers.

- Review zoning regulations for possible restrictions on signage.
- Strategically place plants, trees and decorative accents to obscure unattractive views, shelter customers from the wind and soften noise levels.
- Provide ample lighting to prevent slip-and-fall injuries.
- Keep clear of all debris and shovel in the winter.
- Add handrails along inclines or stairs.
- Provide wheelchair access. Check on local regulations and ADA requirements regarding accessibility for disabled customers.

First Impressions

The exterior and area surrounding your business is vital. Your first priority is getting customers in the door.

- **Parking.** Review the ease of access, traffic flow and available parking when selecting a location. Offer free parking validation.
- **Signage.** Provide attractive and informative signage to "steer" customers to your front door. Post daily specials on a freestanding display by the front door to lure in passersby.
- **Doors.** An attractive "front door" is a powerful welcome and invitation to enter.
- **Storefront.** Differentiate your store from the monochromatic (industrial looks of leased spaces in malls, strip centers and office buildings) with colorful awnings, fresh flower boxes, attractive murals and signs.

- **Music.** Pipe pleasant music throughout the store to set the mood and stimulate buying "appetites."
- **Smells.** Greet customers with positive smells. Fill your landscape with colorful and fragrant flowers, and use pleasant-smelling cleaning products in entryways. Beware of overloading the senses.
- **Flowers.** Fresh flowers represent luxury to many people. Use them in counter displays or near self-serve coffee areas.

Covering Your Floors

Although people might not gush about your flooring, it certainly influences their overall impressions of your store. In a busy environment with heavy foot traffic, flooring choices have lasting consequences and can really overwhelm your design budget.

Here are a few other issues you should consider when selecting flooring materials.

- Choose commercial-grade whenever possible as anticipated usage and lifespan are typically much greater. Check all manufacturers' warranties for coverage in commercial applications.
- Select materials for public areas that won't show scuff marks easily and can handle chairs being dragged across, equipment being wheeled and won't be dented by high-heels.
- Select a medium-colored pattern to hide spots, crumbs and dirt between cleanings.
- Compare hardwood flooring with modern vinyl or acrylic-infused look-alikes. Remember, wood can be sanded and refinished easily while the look-alike would need to be replaced. Select the more expensive strip vinyl flooring for a longer life expectancy than other vinyl products. Replacing small damaged areas is an added benefit.
- Ask your architect about the great ways concrete is being used in

commercial buildings. No, we're not talking about floor that looks like a driveway. New processes and color techniques make this an attractive and durable choice.

- Avoid dark, high-gloss flooring, which show dirt easily, can appear wavy and magnifies any substructure imperfections.
- Make certain all flooring is easy to maintain, can handle chemical exposure, is slip-resistant in wet and dry conditions and meets sanitation code in food prep areas.

Up Above—Ceilings

Ceilings are often overlooked when designing and decorating a store. Customers actually do notice attractive colors, artistic displays and great lighting along with all the dust, cobwebs, stains and ugly ceiling materials. An attractive and clean ceiling tells customers you value cleanliness and care about them.

When choosing ceiling materials, look for sound-deadening materials that are easy to clean and secure tightly to beams, sheetrock or suspension hardware. Below are some things you should know about choosing ceiling materials, designing unique ceilings and maintaining ceilings.

- Transform ceilings with wallpaper, wood paneling, fabric or other suspended treatments. Just be certain all materials are fire-resistant and meet code.
- Use exposed beams, pipes and vents as great color accents and high-tech art pieces. Make certain paint and other treatments are fireproof and heat-resistant for heating and steam pipes, and waterproof for water pipes.
- Reflect more light and make the room feel larger with lighter-colored ceilings. Remember, lighter-colored ceilings will also show venting-related dirt stains.

- Make certain your HVAC is properly vented and well-maintained to eliminate ceiling stains. Lack of maintenance isn't just unsightly, it wastes electricity.
- Incorporate skylights, light tubes and windows to bring in more natural lights. Make certain these can be cleaned easily.
- Think of your ceiling as another wall to be decorated. Tin ceilings, faux painting techniques, mirrors, posters, faux beams, decorative molding and fabric are all potential ways to add drama, carry out a theme or enhance a peaceful environment.

Let There Be Light

Good lightening creates a mood, enhances décor, makes it easier and safer to work and makes you and your products look better. When considering how to light your display cases and service counters, here are some things you will have to consider:

- Level of natural light and seasonal changes that affect it.
- Activities in the room—work areas, walkways, tables, waiting areas.
- Ambiance you desire—bright and simulating, or soft and romantic.
- Artistic and creative uses—the use of light and shadows to accent attractive features or mask less attractive areas.

Lighting effects can be obtained through wall sconces, fiber optics, chandeliers, track lighting, table lamps and directional spotlights.

- Incorporate indirect lighting. Well-placed wall sconces add light without the glare.
- Use color-accurate lighting to enhance the appearances. Incandescent lighting has a warmer, yellow-orange cast; fluorescent lighting produces a blue-green cast—a real appetite-deadener! Halogen lights are closest to true white light.

- Explore full-spectrum lighting (which reportedly make people feel healthier) for work areas.
- Hire a lighting designer. This lighting expert can help you upgrade existing lighting for appearance and energy savings, or design a complete new look.
- Visit GE Lighting online at www.gelighting.com/na/business/retail _solutions.html for design, product selection and energy audits.

A Little Artwork

Think of your products as artwork; use them in creative ways as wall or counter art. Beautiful crystal goblets, cobalt blue toasters and vivid red relishes give you shapes and colors that mimic sculptures. You might offer clocks and art suitable for dining rooms and kitchens. Hand-painted platters can be displayed on easels or decorative canisters featured on lighted pedestals.

Colors That Complement

Color plays an important role in image and brand identification. Scientists have proven that people are affected by the colors surrounding them. Why not incorporate one or two to create the right mood for your store? The chart on the following page list general colors and their emotional connotations.

DECORATING WITH COLORS		
Color	**Connotation**	**Design Notes**
Yellow	Sunlight, cheerful, vitality	Many designers believe every room should have a dash of yellow. Stay away from greenish yellows.
Red	Intensity, passion, stimulates appetites	Use boldly or as an accent.
Blue	Cool, clean and refreshing	Blue should be used away from food as it isn't complementary.
Green	Well-being, nature, fresh and light	Beware—can also make people and food look off-color.
Gold	Wealth and power	Warms up other colors and brightens dark wood.
Neutrals	Masculine—darker browns Feminine—lighter terra cotta shades	Rosy hues make food and people more attractive. Rarely go out of style and provide a background for bold color accents.
White	Clean, fresh and new	Can be a good foundation color but beware: it can also signal institutional, bland, ordinary. Can create glare and eyestrain.
Black	Death and mourning	However, if used properly, black can add elegance and style. Black and white is a classic look. Avoid as a background color, and don't forget that black can show fingerprints and can be difficult to keep looking clean.

Your Restrooms

Providing public restrooms may not be required in your community (unless food is served). If you offer classes or lectures, restrooms are a must. Whether you are required to or voluntarily offer public restrooms, an ample, clean restroom speaks volumes about how you value your customers.

Plumbing and health department standards vary widely across the United States. Also, the Americans with Disabilities Act (ADA) governs accessibility issues for all public places. Be certain that you comply; inadequate restrooms can keep you from opening.

Front-of-the-Store Work Areas

Realistically, not all service work can be accomplished behind closed doors. Here are some different types of work areas you might need in the front-of-the-house. Even if your sole workstation is a long service counter, divide the work area into specific activities. A typical customer counter will need to:

- Display small impulse items.
- Ring up sales.
- Package purchases.
- Take special orders.
- Gift wrap packages.
- Store packaging, clean-up materials and cash register supplies.

Here are some helpful suggestions on designing and implementing front-of-the-store work areas.

- Make them attractive, without sacrificing function.
- Remember, cleanliness and order are important.
- Don't forget to incorporate easy-to-clean surfaces.
- Reduce lifting and carrying with mobile carts and rolling waste receptacles.
- Use properly aimed task lighting to avoid glare while allowing staff full visibility of the work surface.
- Use anti-fatigue mats and non-slip flooring.
- Design work areas to minimize stooping, reaching and lifting.

- Areas should have full view of the store to observe and assist customers.

Senses Check

Regularly walk up to your front door, look around, enter and take in the sights, sounds and smells.

- What catches your eye immediately? First impressions do count!
- Do you feel like this is a clean, well-cared-for establishment?
- Does it feel comfortable and inviting?
- Are you looking at half-filled cans, dripping syrup bottles or ugly trashcans?
- Do you detect the harsh smell of cleanser or the aroma of bread baking?
- Can you hear the counter person over the clanging of pots and pans?

Look for inconsistencies in your message of quality, and correct them immediately. Don't forget to assign someone to make certain that all public areas are kept tidy and inviting throughout the day.

Have fun with your merchandising and decorating—you'll enjoy it and your customers will appreciate it!

Create a Presentation

Displays are your best presentation tool. Your display style should connect with your customers. Most retailers prefer to have their shelves brimming with choices. Empty shelves mean lost sales. However, a minimalist approach where a few items are artfully displayed can be appealing—to the right audience. Your personal presentation style and your customers' needs should be complementary—if not, you won't be happy and neither will they.

Displays aren't just for storage, they are for merchandising. Think presentation, presentation, presentation! Decorate displays for the holidays, add orchids in stem vials, incorporate antiques, use collectible plates or large chargers in food-safe gold with paper doilies, create multiple-level vignettes and angle shelves towards the customer.

Once you get your creative juices flowing, you'll find that merchandising your store can be a great creative outlet that boosts sales!

Window Displays

Window dressing is another creative way to make your store an inviting place to shop. With some basic carpentry tools, a bolt of fabric and some innovative uses for ordinary materials, you can create eye-catching displays.

Keep your window displays tidy and dust-free. Plan on changing them regularly or people will quickly ignore their persuasive power. Mix ordinary items with colorful kitchen utensils. Create theme displays to promote seasonal items.

If you have a broad window ledge, create a diorama by arranging cans or boxes of different sizes and cover them with draping fabric. This multi-level display will make each item stand out. If you don't want people to remove items from the display, create a short barrier that won't block the view. In addition, don't forget to give customers an attractive view from the inside.

Two-sided freestanding displays can be created or purchased to add drama to a window and provide valuable shelving inside. If your store décor has a distinct style or theme, incorporate that into your displays and don't forget to promote holidays and major community events.

Visit your local craft stores, silk flower stores and commercial decorative supply outlets for resources you can incorporate into your various displays.

Shelving

Shelving, as opposed to displays, is primarily storage for activities that take place behind the counter. To improve your counter staff's efficiency, you'll need to store a variety of tools, equipment, supplies and food items within easy reach.

Out of the customers' view, storage units (under the counter or with doors) should be where you keep "unattractive" items such as cash register tape and cleaning supplies. Open shelving facing the customer can be artfully arranged for appearance and functionality. You'll need to balance functionality with appearance and orderliness. (More information on displays and store fixtures can be found in Chapter 12.)

14

Back-of-the-Store Work Areas

Beyond public areas, there are other rooms or work areas that directly affect your productivity. Properly handling incoming deliveries, storing merchandise and supplies, conducting employee reviews and dealing with the waste can even boost your profitability.

Delivery Areas

Whether your facility has a loading dock or just a back access door, it is important that you have the equipment and procedures to accept, log in and prepare incoming shipments for storage. When selecting vendors, inquire about their delivery service. How do they package heavy bulk items? Will they just drop everything at the door, or will they move bulky boxes to storage areas for you?

Below are some recommendations on outfitting your delivery area:

- Don't forget to provide employees with protective gear such as gloves and smocks.

- Having computer access in this area can speed check-in. Packing slips can be quickly compared with orders, accepted and signed off. However, a clipboard with copies of orders can suffice.

- Create a procedural manual. Each vendor has a damaged goods and return policy; keep copies of these in your binder for quick reference.

Your employees should understand proper delivery acceptance procedures. Below are some procedures they must know to catch ordering errors and vendor shipment errors.

- All visibly damaged merchandise must be noted on packing slips or bills of lading (or depending upon the vendor's recommendations, refused). This helps the vendor file third-party carrier claims.

- Hidden damage should be noted on the packing slip and management advised immediately so claims can be filed.

- Products should be inspected for package damage, signs of pests and excess debris and mishandling.

- Overages or shortages should likewise be noted on the packing slips or bills of lading.

- Employees must sanitize their hands and remove soiled aprons to avoid potential cross-contamination with opened goods.

- Realize that the delivery person may not be at fault. Take your complaints to the vendor's customer service department or your sales representative.

Storage

You'll have short-term and long-term storage needs. Short-term storage is for merchandise back stock that will be used to refill shelves and supplies that need quick replenishing. Long-term storage would be for seasonal decorations and early-buy products that won't be introduced in the store for several weeks.

Before you can determine your storage needs, you'll need to review the amount of back stock you'll have at any time. Knowing what and when you'll be purchasing will help you make better storage choices.

Increase productivity by creating three types of storage.

- **Active.** Accessed repeatedly throughout the day. Located closest to the active work area.

- **Back-up.** Back-up merchandise and supplies for active areas used occasionally during one week. Located further from the active work area but easily accessible.

- **Long-term.** Non-perishable special-use and seasonal items. Uses out-of-reach, back of the building, under stairs and less accessible areas.

Below are some practical ideas on creating useful storage areas.

- All shelving should be at least 6 inches from the floor to deter pests.

- Make storage cabinets in public areas attractive, a part of the décor and from materials that clean easily.

- Create separate (but convenient) storage for chemical cleaners and other hazardous materials. Check your local regulations regarding hazardous material storage.

- Evaluate all storage for potential cross-contamination issues. This includes chemicals, foodstuff and handling methods.

- Incorporate easily movable or sectional storage whenever possible to maximize layout flexibility.

- Protect employees from injury by placing heavy items closest to waist-height as possible. Provide sturdy stepstools, ladders and rolling carts nearby. Except for rarely accessed areas, keep shelving shallow enough for easy reach.

Refrigeration

Your refrigeration requirements may be limited to your employee's lunches. However, if you have back stock that requires refrigeration, invest in commercial models. Consumer models do not provide as even a temperature or ample room. Look for a model that provides you with sufficient space to hold serving trays of samples and fresh ingredients to be used during cooking demonstrations.

Freezer

You may not have to invest in a freezer. However, you may find that quick-frozen fruits or vegetables are a better choice than inferior off-season goods for some uses. As with refrigerators, allow ample space so food will chill faster.

Waste and Recycling

Handling food, oil/grease and solid waste takes time, effort and money. Waste management and reduction are not only cost-effective, they are wise environmental and business choices. Here are some helpful ideas on managing and reducing your store waste and disposal costs:

- **Purchase a waste disposal unit.** Look for stainless steel units with automatic reversal controls. Select units with ample horsepower and rotor size to handle your typical food waste. Invest in long-term performance when comparison shopping.

- **Build a recycling center and establish a usage program.** Include recycling equipment in your back-of-the-house layout. Contact recycling/waste companies about pickup programs. Make it easy for employees to comply by incorporating sorting bins and conveniently located waste receptacles. Install color-coded recycling containers on wheels. Be prepared to handle large quantities of paper, cardboard, plastics, glass and metal waste. Cardboard balers, for example, can pay for themselves through reduced hauling costs.

- **Invest in a commercial-grade trash compactor.** Even with the most aggressive recycling program, you will still have trash. A compactor will pay for itself quickly by maximizing bin use and minimizing hauling fees.

Your Office

Every business needs an office. If you choose to handle your book work at home, you should still have an in-house office. This can be an entire room or an isolated work area. You'll need ample lighting (natural or artificial), filing cabinets (including locking cabinets) and a suitable desk and chair. Your computer could be a single workstation or part of your store's computerized network.

- Create an organized and productive work area so others, in your absence, can locate, file and process paperwork.
- Store confidential documents in locked filing cabinets.
- Keep copies of all policy and procedural manuals available for reference.

The investments you make in creating a work environment that protects your employees, your customers and your community will reward your business with increased productivity and savings.

15

Creating a Safe and Productive Business and Work Environment

The investments you make in creating a work environment that protects your employees, your customers and your community will reward your business with increased productivity and savings. This chapter will address a variety of productivity, safety and security issues. Beyond the typical retailer's considerations, businesses that sell food products must also be concerned with proper handling, storage and potential package tampering.

Food Safety and Security

If you are preparing or serving any food or beverage, you will need to follow accepted food safety measures. Whether you offer coffee samples or have an olive oil tasting, you and your staff should be trained in proper food-handling and sanitation procedures. Your local health department can guide you through these (even if you are not required to obtain a food service license or are subject to inspections). Following are a few useful food safety tips:

- Use toothpicks, disposable spoons, forks, paper plates and cups when serving samples.
- Provide single-serving condiment packages (sugar, salt, etc.) whenever possible to avoid contamination.
- Provide ample napkins, trashcans and disposable wet towels to keep hands clean.
- Assign one person to handle samples to avoid cross-contamination during money-handling and other activities. Keep water-free antibacterial cleaners handy.
- Use a sneeze guard when and where required by your local health department.
- Make your sample process interactive so your sales staff can close the sale and discourage "double dippers."

Food Security

Unfortunately, the world has become a place where business owners need to consider things like package tampering and product adulteration. The FDA has a retailer's guide to food security issues at http://vm.cfsan.fda.gov/~dms/secguid5.html. Below are a few tips to ensure your customers' safety.

- Never leave incoming shipments unattended in the delivery area.
- Reject all visibly damaged boxes upon receipt.
- Inspect all packaging, including seals, when stocking shelves and periodically while dusting.
- Report any visible powders, residues, staining or leakage to the manufacturer and/or authorities.
- Restrict access to food preparation and storage areas.
- Store and lock chemicals away from food preparation or storage areas.

Protecting Your Customers and Employees

Sharp knives, heavy pots, hanging displays, beautiful glass bowls and coffee samples are all potential hazards for your customers. Cuts, slips, falls, pinched fingers and smashed toes are all possible in your store. Your responsibility is to provide an environment that provides as much protection as possible. As you design your store layout, stock your shelves and create eye-catching displays, you must consider the potential for customer injury. You can do this by providing:

- Aisles wide enough so heavy coats, full arms and wheelchairs don't catch or sweep items off shelves.
- Attractive slip-resistant mats by all doors and "wet" areas.
- Shelving that is properly anchored to walls and floors.
- Freestanding displays that are well balanced to avoid tipping.
- Displayed items where components won't drop off or separate when picked up (e.g., lids, handles).
- Ladders with locking wheels for hard-to-reach items. These are for employee use only—never let a customer climb these.

Kid-Proof

Your store offers dozens of tantalizing products—especially for inquisitive children. Unfortunately, parents can be too lax when it comes to watching them while shopping. This means you'll have to accept some responsibility for keeping dangerous items out of reach. Keep breakable, easy-to-swallow and sharp items away from lower shelves. Protect your youngest visitors by:

- Locking lower storage doors.
- Covering electrical outlets with safety caps.
- Setting hot samples away from traffic areas and on stable surfaces.

A First-Rate Facility

A safe and sanitary environment begins with a facility that is clean and in good repair. The entire facility—work areas as well as equipment—should be designed for easy cleaning and maintenance. It's important to eliminate hard-to-clean work areas and get rid of dirty surroundings and any conditions that will attract pests. Remember, the easier the workplace is to clean, the more likely it will stay clean.

Bugs, Insects and Animal Pests

Bug, insect and rodent infestation is the result of poor sanitation practices. Aside from being a nuisance, they are a health threat. Pests require three necessities for life: food, water and warmth. Eliminate the environment that these pests need to live, and you will be eliminating their existence. Combining proper sanitation practices with periodic food-safe extermination will stop any problems before they start.

All doorjambs and building cracks, even the thinnest ones, must be sealed. Be cautious when receiving deliveries. Bugs may be in the boxes or crates. To prevent the spread of flies in your establishment:

- Keep all doors, windows and screens closed at all times.
- Ensure that garbage is sealed in airtight containers and is picked up regularly. All trash must be cleaned off the ground; flies can deposit their eggs on the thinnest scrap of food.
- Dumpsters must be periodically steam cleaned and deodorized. They should never contain any decaying food scraps.

The greatest protection against cockroaches is your exterminator. Of course, the exterminator will be of little value if you do not already have good sanitary practices in place. Select an exterminator who is currently servicing other retail stores. Chemicals sprayed inside your store should be of the non-residual type. These are safe and approved for use in food service establishments.

Animal pests, such as rats and mice, can be a very serious and destructive problem. Rodents are prolific breeders, producing as many as 50 offspring in a lifespan of one year. They tend to hide during the day, but their telltale signs can reveal their presence. They are extremely strong and can easily gain access to a building through a crack or hole no larger than a quarter. Ensure that your building's foundation is airtight. Keep all food products at least 6 inches off the floor; this enables the exterminator to get under the shelving to spray. Rat bait, a poisoning capsule resembling food, is particularly effective when spread around the building and dumpsters. As with any poison or chemical you use, make certain that it is labeled clearly and stored away from food-storage areas.

Fires

Fire extinguishers should be available in the front and back of the store. All employees should be trained in avoiding fires as well as in the use of fire extinguishers and in evacuation procedures. Always call the fire department first, before using a fire extinguisher!

Wash Areas

Your wash-up area most likely will be your employee restroom. This room should be stocked with antibacterial soap and paper towels (these are more sanitary than other hand-drying methods), and surface areas should be sanitized daily. To avoid cross-contamination, consider faucets and soap dispensers that are hands-free (elbow or foot control). All employees must be properly trained in hand-washing procedures to minimize transmission of illness and germs.

Storage Areas

Keeping your storage areas clean and clutter-free will help you prevent accidents and discourage pests. You'll also have other benefits such as being able to find things quickly and keeping resale merchandise in good condition. Provide ample lighting, sturdy ladders and a non-slip walk surface to prevent on-the-job injuries.

Good Ergonomics

Ergonomics is the study and engineering of human physical interaction with spaces and objects during activities. A prep area that requires workers to repeatedly stretch across to reach tools that only very tall workers can safely reach is an example of "poor" ergonomics.

Good ergonomic design can positively affect your employees' physical well being, safety, productivity and comfort. Good ergonomics, such as the right height counters and comfortable chairs, can also enhance your customers' experience.

Here are some valuable tips to help you "engineer" your store to work well with people.

- Create body-friendly work areas where supplies are readily at hand, desks are the proper height and chairs fit the user.
- Eliminate excessive bending, lifting, and reaching while encouraging proper stocking and storage procedures.
- Make certain your tools and equipment weren't designed for only specific body types. Accommodating shorter frames, smaller hands or differing physical characteristics increases productivity and minimizes health risks.
- Purchase a supply of important tools and utensils for left-handed employees.
- Think about how employees, customers and vendors will interact with your facility. Does the facility or equipment make it easier or more difficult to do their job or enjoy their shopping experience?

It's Good to Be Green

In building and/or renovating your retail facility, you have an opportunity to incorporate green materials and designs. Look for grants, low-interest loans and funding for green construction. See:

- Funding Green Buildings, www.fundinggreenbuildings.com, are funding consultants specializing in green building.

- ShoreBank Pacific offers eco-loans for Pacific Northwest businesses. You can find information at www.eco-bank.com.

- Fat Earth, www.fatearth.com, offers a financing resource directory and other information on paying for energy-saving and green construction and equipment.

Here are some resources to learn more about creating a less wasteful and more ecologically productive business.

- **Hire green building professionals.** A service directory can be found at Greenbuilder.com, www.greenbuilder.com, or search Yahoo's Business Directory by the keywords "green building."

- **Pick up a book on the subject.** As this is a rapidly changing industry, select the newest books available. Popular titles include:
  - *Green Building Handbook: A Companion Guide to Building Products and Their Impact on the Environment* by Tom Wolley.

  - *Green Building Materials: A Guide to Product Selection and Specification* by Ross Spiegel and Dru Meadows.

- **Require your architect and builder to comply with the EPA's Energy Star Design Target program.** Details at http://208.254.22.6/index.cfm?c=business.bus_index.

- **Research sustainable and green resources** at Fat Earth, www.fatearth.com.

- **Use your green building efforts as a springboard for free local and regional publicity.** Register your building and efforts with the EPA's Energy Star Program. Contact your utility company and explore joint PR opportunities.

Conserving Energy

Environmental systems (lighting, heating, cooling and ventilation) require an enormous amount of energy—typically 30 to 50 percent of your annual energy cost. Energy-conscious construction methods, along with energy-efficient equipment and environmental systems, are wise investments. Although initial costs may be greater, your ROI could actually offset the full cost of the equipment over its lifespan. Below we've detailed some useful tips to help you create an energy-wise store.

- Have your local utility company complete a free energy assessment on your existing facility. They can monitor the efficiency of systems to help you determine your actual energy cost per month for each. Use these figures to compute potential energy savings if you replaced the HVAC units with more efficient models.

- Don't overlook small ways to save, such as more efficient light bulbs, programmable thermostats and double-paned insulated windows.

- Visit www.energystar.gov/smallbiz to learn about the EPA's Energy Star program designed to help small businesses become more energy efficient.

- Seek out private and government lenders who specialize in financing energy-related improvements for the most favorable interest rates.

- Contact your utility companies about subsidies, rebates and financial incentives for replacing inefficient equipment with approved models. Your tax accountant can also advise you on state or federal tax incentives.

- Hire an energy consultant to make recommendations on your design and equipment choices.

- Remember, you are investing in your bottom-line with long-term payoffs for your store and our environment. Energy costs have historically risen, so your savings factor could be even more significant in future years.

The Air We Breath

Healthy air, inside and out, is a business and moral concern that impacts stores legally and fiscally. "Poor air" contributes directly to employee absenteeism and unhappy customers. Many communities have rigid air emission and work environment regulations relating to proper ventilation, wood burning, grease and smoke. Unpleasant odors also contribute to "poor" air quality.

Fresh Indoor Air

Indoor air quality requires bringing sufficient outdoor air in, properly filtering the outdoor and recirculated air and directing airflow. Often our efforts to save energy has created a new problem called "sealed" building syndrome where building materials, emissions and other chemicals become a greater health risk.

Below are several examples of helpful tips on improving indoor air quality.

- Ban employee smoking in the entire building. The smell of smoke certainly isn't stimulating for customers, and smoke doesn't know that it is supposed to stay in one area.

- Install a whole-building air cleaner/filtration system that also reduces airborne particles and dust.

- Check for radon, mold spores and biological dangers when converting older or long-vacant buildings.

- Read what the EPA says about indoor air quality at www.epa.gov /iaq/pubs/insidest.html.

- Be aware of unhealthy emissions from carpeting, paint and cleaning products. Sick Building Syndrome is explained at the National Safety Council site (www.nsc.org/ehc/indoor/sbs.htm).

- Hire an HVAC contractor or engineer with retail experience. Hire contractors to install new systems or maintain existing systems and an engineer to design and specify systems.

Drinking Water

In some communities, your tap water isn't very appetizing. Unsavory odors and harsh tastes along with hard water deposits are common issues. Unseen bacteria and pollutants may also be a concern. Poor water can adversely affect your food or beverage quality and damage equipment. If you use water, a filtration or reverse osmosis system can be a wise investment.

Below are some additional tips on offering your customers clean, fresh and tasty water.

- Determine what's in your water. Your water department or independent testing company can provide your water's composition (solids, hardness, chlorine levels). Select equipment that addresses your water's "bad" elements. Besides safe and tasty water, your specific chemical and equipment needs for washing produce, equipment and dishware are affected by your water's composition.

- Look for filtration systems that can be easily cleaned or use inexpensive replaceable filters. Filters should be ample enough for a 6-month maintenance cycle.

- Don't overlook clean, filtered water for icemakers.

- Choose systems that can reduce chlorine levels to approximately .5 parts per million for the best tasting coffee and tea.

- Sell high-profit sparkling and still bottled water. Some customers prefer the "safety" and convenience of bottled water.

16

Your Store Staff

Every store is unique in the way it operates. In a small, independent store, your staff will probably handle a broad range of duties with each working for a common goal. Before you hire your first employee, it is important that you write a job description. Remember, you cannot find the right person for the job if you don't really know what that job will entail.

Retail Operations Manager

As a small-business owner, you may fill the duties of an operations manager. In larger retail operations, you may find that hiring an operations manager increases your productivity and provides you with a trusted employee who can provide backup and share duties. Operations managers are responsible for:

- Hiring, training, supervising and scheduling employees.
- Establishing and maintaining stocking levels.
- Controlling waste.
- Ordering, receiving and storing all products.
- Setting, training and enforcing health and safety regulations.
- Keeping the owner informed of possible problem areas.

- Acting as media contact.
- Enhancing employee communications and morale.

Customer Service Staff

Your full- and part-time customer service staff are the people who can set your business apart from your competition. Part-time employees are an excellent resource during peak times. Look for employees who share your passion for food. People who enjoy their job will make you and your customers happier. Your staff will:

- Make your customers feel welcome.
- Offer advice on food, equipment and tools.
- Sell products and services by promotion, advice and demonstration.
- Research and process special orders.
- Handle cash and credit transactions.

Teacher/Demonstrator

The best way to sell more is to show people how to use what you sell. Having experts on cooking, baking, cake decorating, wine, coffee, tea and entertaining "on the payroll" can be a valuable investment. Depending upon your store, you may find having a coordinator or teacher to handle these tasks can keep people coming in regularly to see and learn more.

Below are a few other ways to have experts "on call":

- Contact manufacturers regarding traveling demonstrators and sales reps.

- Collaborate with complementary retailers. Work with other gourmet food businesses and "share" customers. Everyone benefits! If you sell barbecues, join forces with a local butcher. If you sell elegant linens and tableware, have a caterer talk about how to throw a formal party. If you sell sushi-making supplies, feature a fishmonger's wares.

- Speak to hospitality/restaurant schools to locate students interested in using your store to improve their skills.
- Partner with a local cooking school.
- Develop a relationship with farmers and ranchers interested in promoting their products locally.

Cashier

Separating money-handling duties from other customer service responsibilities can make it easier to be waited on. Some customers prefer to find what they need and pay quickly; others enjoy lengthy visits, and others will need some one-on-one consultation and advice. Having a cashier who isn't working the floor can free up your more experienced staff and help you meet everyone's needs. A cashier must be able to:

- Handle cash, checks and credit card transactions quickly and efficiently.
- Provide support to other employees while prioritizing customer interactions.
- Handle phone calls without inconveniencing the person at the register.
- Contact customers regarding special order arrivals and deliveries.

Stocking/Inventory Assistants

Having someone to handle incoming shipments and keeping shelves stocked can be a wise investment. Other staff members will probably handle these duties in smaller stores. Stock assistants would:

- Handle receiving, logging-in and storing incoming inventory and supplies.

- Maintain waste and recycling programs.
- Be responsible for regularly inventorying consumables, such as paper towels, toilet paper, cups, etc.
- Replace resale items that have been removed by customers and other employees.
- Restock shelves to maintain desired display levels.
- Dust and adjust displays, shelving and wall units.

17

Purchasing

The goal of purchasing is to supply the store with the best goods, services and supplies at the lowest possible cost. You must have favorable working relations with your suppliers and vendors. A large amount of time will be spent meeting with prospective sales representatives and companies. Your responsibility is to evaluate and decide how to best make each of the purchases for the store.

Purchasing is a complex area that must be managed by someone who is completely familiar with customer interests and needs and the store's needs. One person (and a trained backup) should handle all purchasing for the store. There are several advantages to this including greater negotiating power and better overall control.

Before a Single Item Is Purchased

You need to refresh yourself with your 25-word business description, your demographic research and your customer profile. Every item you purchase for resale should fit into the description, be priced appropriately and be of interest to your ideal customer.

During your research period, you may have attended one of dozens of regional and national trade shows that offer products suitable for your store. Perhaps you have visited a gift mart in a major city. Gift marts are typically located in warehouse districts and are filled with rep groups, distributors and manufacturers wholesaling a broad range of products, including gourmet foods, specialty linens and other upscale items. Retail display marts can also be found around the country, filled with displays, shelving and signage for retail operations.

Create Wish Lists

A good place to start in stocking your shelves is to create wish lists—a list for resale items, display/marketing materials and supplies.

- Develop a list of types of items you want to resell, and include brand names whenever important. Add sources for each.
- Write a second list that details how you will store, display and market your resale goods.
- Start a list for all the various supplies (these are typically consumable items) that your store will need to operate every day. Keep this list handy so you can jot down items as they come up during your business launch.

Working with Vendors

Few major manufacturers work directly with independent retail stores. This means you'll most likely work with an authorized distributor and/or manufacturer's rep group. If you have a specific manufacturer in mind, check their Web site for your local contact. Smaller manufacturers are more apt to have wholesale programs based upon smaller minimum buys. (You'll also find resources for locating brand names and products within select categories in Chapter 12.)

Many fine gourmet items are imported. An established manufacturer or food producer often has an import relationship with an American distributor. Unless you are interested in learning the ins and outs of importing goods, rely on their expertise to ensure that all national security inspections, country of origin documentation and other state and federal paperwork have been handled. If you are interested in traveling abroad to seek out products for your shop, locate an international wholesale trade directory and make arrangements before you leave to visit factories and exporters.

The Web reaches well beyond our shores so try searching by product types to locate foreign-made goods. When looking at Web site addresses (their URL) look for country codes (like the .com [dot com], such as .nz for New Zealand or .it for Italy). For a list of country codes, check a site like Bit Media at www.bitmedia.com/cc/url1.htm.

Ask and You Shall Receive

Although you might be a big customer, don't be shy about asking for buying terms, co-op advertising, dating and other perks or discounts. "Is this the best price I can get for these?" is a very powerful question. As a new customer and/or a new business, you aren't necessarily in a strong position. You may be required to start out on a COD or prepaid basis. However, if you let your salesperson know that you want to build a strong relationship and establish a good credit rating, you can earn many of these benefits. This is one of the best reasons to pay your bills promptly and don't over-extend yourself.

Manufacturers are interested in getting their products sold so many offer:

- Seasonal dating where you place orders well before the specific season, receive them on time to fill your shelves and pay for them after the season is over and after you've made your profit. Nothing like making money on someone else's investment!

- Extended terms are those beyond the vendor's standard net 15- or net 30-day terms; typically this would be extended to 45 or 60 days. Again, this can be a great way to maximize your resources. Beware of penalties for late payment, and don't forget to pay on time.

- Buy one, get one promotions are used by manufacturers just as you might in your store. However, even if you get one free, you still have stocking and overhead costs for storage. Or perhaps the freebie is just a way to move something from their warehouse to yours.

- Co-op advertising is short for cooperative advertising. This is where a manufacturer sponsors or provides funds to you for the sole purpose of promoting their products. The amount available to you is typically a percentage of your purchases. Co-op plans are a win-win situation; however, you must comply with the rules to receive the benefits.

- Displays, dispensers and merchandising products are items furnished at no charge, at deep discounts or available through co-op plans. Often manufacturers want a "unified" look for retail displays and have a variety of temporary or permanent merchandisers for your use.

The key is to ask for these! Don't leave it up to the salesperson to tell you what is available. Be certain to enroll yourself in any "frequent buyer" programs, customer newsletters and other communications that might keep you informed of new products, promotions and retailer benefits.

Ordering Procedures

The foundation of solid ordering procedures is inventory control. Analyzing turnaround times will help you determine stocking quantities.

A single person should be responsible for ordering all products and supplies. However, empowering employees to discuss what is needed and why, can give you insights that no computer can.

Ordering on set days will help you keep the task under control. Issue purchase orders and keep copies of these in the receiving area for reference at delivery time. If there are any special shipping/handling procedures, be certain to include these so your staff is aware of the situation.

Inventory Levels

The first step in computing what item and how much of it to order is to determine your minimum and maximum inventory levels. Your minimum level is your signal to reorder before you run out. Understanding your daily, weekly or monthly usage and delivery turnaround will help you keep the proper quantity on hand. Your maximum inventory level keeps your buyer from buying too much standing inventory. This process, often called "just-in-time" inventory, is your goal. Tying up valuable cash can limit your ability to pay expenses and negate any volume purchase discount you may receive.

To determine the amount you need to order, you must take a physical inventory on a regular basis. You may also rely on computerized inventory systems as a basis for purchasing; however, an actual count should be taken at least at the end of every quarter. Handheld UPC code readers tied to inventory systems can be a real time saver.

To determine the "Desired Inventory," you will need to know when regularly scheduled deliveries arrive for that item and the amount used in the period between deliveries. Add on about 25 percent to the average amount used; this will cover unexpected usage, a late delivery or a backorder at the vendor.

The amount you need to order is the difference between the "Desired Inventory Level" and the amount "On Hand." Experience and food demand will reveal the amount an average order should contain.

A buying schedule should be set up and adhered to. This would consist of a calendar showing:

- Which day's orders need to be placed?
- When deliveries will be arriving.
- What items will be arriving from which company.
- Contact information for customer service and/or sales representatives for each vendor.

- The price the sales representative quoted or other special pricing/ discounts.

Post the buying schedule on the office wall. When a delivery doesn't arrive as scheduled, you should call the company immediately. Don't wait until the end of the day when offices are closed.

A Want Sheet may be placed on a clipboard under the front counter. This sheet is made available for employees to write in any items customers may want you to stock, need for a special order or to do their jobs more efficiently. This is a very effective form of communication and employees should be encouraged to use it.

Receiving and Storing

Deliveries will be arriving throughout the day by UPS, USPS and freight carriers. Receiving and storing each product is a critical responsibility. A staff member who was not properly trained in the correct procedures can make costly mistakes. A slight inaccuracy on an invoice or improper storing of a perishable item could cost the store hundreds of dollars.

All products delivered to the store must be:

- Inspected for visible damage. Depending upon the shipper's policy, either refuse the shipment or have the delivery person make note of all damage. The shipper and the shipping company set freight damage claim requirements.

- Checked against the actual order sheet for the exact specification ordered (weight, size, quantity).

- Accompanied by an invoice containing: current price, totals, date, company name and receiver's signature. Noted for discrepancies on bills of lading and other related paperwork.

- Opened and checked for overages and shortages.

- Reviewed for accurate COD amount.

- Dated, rotated and put in the proper storage area immediately. Locked in their storage areas securely.

- Keep an invoice box handy to store all invoices and packing slips received during the day. Prior to leaving for the day, the receiver must bring the invoices to the manager's office and place them in a designated spot.

Rotation Procedures

- Older items move to the front and to the left. In any part of the store, the first item used should always be the oldest.

- Date and label all items. An office self-inking date stamp is handy, or code your price stickers.

Issuing

Some items are purchased in bulk but only a few are displayed or used at a time. You may find a system for "issuing" these items is a valuable part of inventory control. Create a Sign-out Sheet that includes all items that you will issue to employees. The Sign-out Sheet should be on a clipboard near the storage unit. When a part of a case or box is removed, the quantity removed must be recorded. The signing-out procedure will eliminate pilferage and help you create waste-reduction procedures.

Products such as restroom or cleaning supplies may be issued in a similar manner. If these or other items were being stolen, the cost of each would show up in the cost projections at the end of the month.

Simple manual systems can be created using predesigned forms that are worked with daily. Many basic purchasing and receiving functions are found in retail inventory and accounting programs.

Identifying Inventory Theft

Check the invoices every day for the items delivered that are in your inventory. Ensure that all items signed off as being delivered are actually in the storage areas. Should there be a discrepancy, check with the employee that signed the invoice. The number of items you start with plus the number you received in deliveries, minus the amount signed out by your assigned staff, must equal the number on hand. If there is a discrepancy, you may have a thief.

If you suspect a theft in the store, record the names of all employees who worked that particular shift. If thefts continue to occur, a pattern will develop among the employees who were working on all the days in question. Compute the perpetual inventory or other controls you are having a problem with at different times of the day, before and after each shift. This will pinpoint the area and shift in which the theft is occurring. Sometimes, placing a notice to all employees that you are aware of a theft problem in the store will resolve the problem. Make it clear that any employee caught stealing will be terminated immediately.

18

Cash Flow

Daily involvement and analysis of your financial records are necessary if the store is to take full advantage of the credit terms and discounts offered by suppliers. Substantial savings can be acquired simply by managing the store's cash flow and utilizing its purchasing power.

After you've been operating for a few months, most purveyors will extend 30-day net terms if you request them. This is an advantageous situation; through proper management, the store's inventory may be turned over as many as five or six times in a 30-day period. In effect, the purveyors will be financing your operations. Few businesses can turn their inventories over this quickly, so they are forced to pay interest or finance charges. Quick turnover is one of the blessings of the retail business. Careful planning and synchronization between the purchasing and bookkeeping departments are needed to obtain maximum utilization of the cash flow. The savings are well worth the additional effort.

CODs and Your Cash Flow

It is not uncommon for vendors to require payment upon delivery (this is especially true for new businesses). The best tracking procedure is to have a check ready. However, small deliveries can be paid "from the till" by an authorized employee. You'll need to take extra precautions with this procedure. A memo form should be filled out with the particulars and placed in the till so that the assigned cashier can properly balance at the end of their shift. Employees must be extra careful when accepting COD deliveries because your "leverage" in problem-solving and the sense of urgency is diminished with a vendor who has already been paid.

Being Paid

Customers will be paying you with cash, travelers' checks, company or personal checks, debit cards (ATM) and credit cards. Additionally, you may receive (after issuing) gift cards, store vouchers for returns, rain checks and discount coupons, all of which need to be handled similar to cash/credit to balance the register. Cash has a low risk factor (counterfeit bills) and requires little more than depositing it into the bank. Checks have a medium risk factor (stolen checks and non-sufficient funds) with related handling fees. Debit and credit cards have a medium risk factor (stolen cards) and on-going processing fees and expenses.

Cash-Handling

Proper cash-handling procedures are critical. Below are some helpful cash-handling, sales-reporting and auditing procedural tips.

- If possible, individual cash drawers should be available for each cashier. This will help you determine if someone isn't handling the duty accurately. Computerized systems can have specific coded keys to keep tallies separate.

- Cash drawers should be prepared and assigned each morning. The responsible cashier should recount the drawer's contents and sign a receipt for the funds.

- At the end of each shift, the responsible cashier should count and balance their drawer against the cash register's report.

- All overages or shortages should be written up and signed off by a supervisor. Drawers are "checked" back into the safe with the responsible supervisor.
- Checks and credit card receipts should be tallied separately and stored in the safe until the bookkeeper is ready to deposit them.
- Automated credit card processing can be a real time saver, and you'll receive the funds faster.
- For made-to-order items, use sequentially numbered guest checks and/or custom product forms. Maintain control over these to monitor potential employee fraud. Voided guest checks should be kept and turned in at the end of the day.
- For phone or Web orders, make certain the credit card's 4-digit ID code is listed.
- For in-person purchases, write the customer's phone number on the form. If an error is made, you'll be able to contact the customer.
- Set up a cash reserve or special account and reimburse the cash drawer for this "Cash Paid Out." When the check from the credit card company comes in, put the "Paid Out" amount back into the reserve or special account.

Counterfeit Bills

Your bank's loss-prevention department can assist you with properly identifying counterfeit currency and provide you with training materials. There are also counterfeit money detector pens to assist you.

Foreign Currency

Depending upon your store's location and tourist trade, you may need to be able to handle foreign currency. Obviously, stores near the Mexican or Canadian border or located in an airport will be seeing international currency and will need more extensive procedures. Again, your bank can provide you with guidelines. Daily currency exchange rate charts can be downloaded from the Internet and some POS systems can even be programmed to handle these automatically.

Foreign-issued credit cards will automatically pay you in U.S. dollars while charging the card holder the appropriate exchange rate.

Travelers' Checks

Most banks handle incoming travelers' checks as they would any other check. Check with your bank on any special handling requirements or fees. Be certain to train your employees on the proper method of accepting travelers' checks, such as requiring that they be signed in front of them, asking for identification and checking your "bad check" list.

Checks

Develop a check acceptance policy and make certain employees know how to follow it without making your customers feel like they are going through an FBI investigation. Typically, you would never accept bank starter kit checks, non-imprinted checks or third-party checks. You might not accept "out of town" checks. Your bank's loss-protection department can provide you with training tools on accepting checks. Familiarize yourself on your state's "bad check" laws and follow these carefully to protect your rights in collecting and/or prosecuting people who pass these.

There are a variety of "immediate" acceptance and confirm systems available to help you reduce bad check losses. Check Fraud (www.checkfraud.com)

offers valuable advice online.

Remember, upscale stores can be better targets than a thrift store for fraud so be diligent without being offensive. Don't post ugly "we prosecute" signs, but do make clear your acceptance and return policies when paying by check.

Debit and Credit Cards

Debit cards (also known as ATM cards) and credit cards are different legal instruments of payment. Debit cards are funds transfer cards while credit cards are funds issued against lines of credit. Laws regarding collection are different: hence your risk, the bank's risk and the credit card companies' risk is different. Your bank will typically charge you more for processing and handling credit card (signature) transactions.

Other Forms of Payment

Various other forms of payment are typically those you have sold or issued to customers. Gift card/certificates have become exceptionally popular as they are the gift certain to "fit" everyone. These have a cash value; although you have already received payment for these. Outstanding gift cards and gift certificates will be tallied and tracked as they are an asset and a future obligation to you.

Store vouchers may be issued during a merchandise return. These vouchers need to be logged and monitored. Rain checks and other discount transactions should be used as an offset for the current price. While not true "cash" transactions, they need to be handled so you can keep track of the activity.

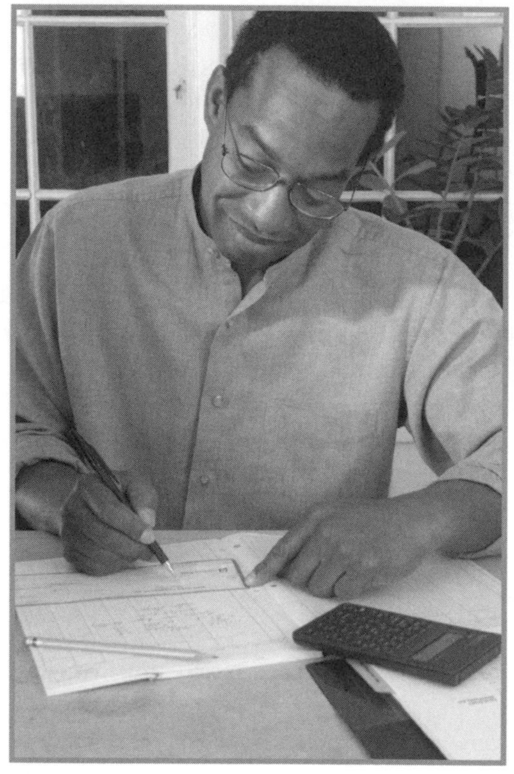

Your involvement in compiling, reporting and analyzing the financial data is critical to your ability to react quickly to problems, invest wisely and grow your business.

19

Financial Management and Budgeting

Internal bookkeeping is where all financial transactions may be tallied, analyzed and reconciled. Your involvement in compiling, reporting and analyzing the financial data is critical to your ability to react quickly to problems, invest wisely and grow your business.

You should allot a couple of hours of each day to accounting. For many businesspeople, hiring a skilled part-time bookkeeper is a wise investment. The bookkeeper's primary responsibility is to ensure that all sales, invoices and bills are accurately recorded and balanced. It is recommended that the bookkeeper not be used in any other capacity in the store, as he or she will be auditing the money and work of the other employees. The bookkeeper must understand and appreciate the confidential nature and importance of the work he or she is doing.

Your CPA should be used from time to time to audit the records, prepare financial and tax statements and lend management advisory services.

To locate a certified bookkeeper in your area, visit the American Institute of

Professional Bookkeepers at http://aipb.org. If you cannot find an in-house bookkeeper, a neighborhood bookkeeping service can assist you.

Accounting Software

QuickBooks® by Intuit is a popular accounting package for the small business. QuickBooks (www.quickbooks.com) is rich in features including built-in remote-access capabilities and Web interfaces. Payroll and retail inventory modules are also available along with the coordinating tax program, TurboTax, for individuals and sole proprietorships. Through Intuit, you can locate a local, authorized QuickBooks consultant and accounting specialist to assist you with using this program.

Another popular accounting package is Peachtree (www.peachtree.com). Peachtree, like QuickBooks, offers an assortment of features and more than one version.

There are also QuickBooks- and Peachtree-certified accountants and bookkeepers that can assist you with setting up your accounting system and work directly with your files.

Your accountant can also give you his or her recommendations or you can check the free service by CPA Online at www.findaccountingsoftware .com. In addition, several of the retail management software packages above offer accounting (accounts receivable, accounts payable and inventory) components. (Additional information on computers and software can be found in Chapter 12.)

Budgeting

To be financially successful, you must set up a long-range plan detailing how much money you want the store to return and when. Budgeting is an accounting record and a tool used to evaluate how effectively the store, management and employees performed during the month. Reviewing this information will help you recognize cost problem areas and act quickly to correct them. We recommend you use a monthly budget because of the fluctuating operating performances common in establishments.

Monthly Budgeting

Once set up and operating, about four hours each month is all that will be required to compute the old budget and project a new one. Although the store may only be in the pre-opening stage, it is imperative that you start to develop an operating budget now. As soon as the budget is prepared, you will possess the control for guiding the business towards your financial goal.

There are many other benefits to preparing and adhering to a monthly operational budget.

- Supervisors and key employees will develop increased awareness and concern about the store and controlling its costs.
- A well-structured, defined budget and orderly financial records will aid you greatly in obtaining loans, and will develop an important store of information should you decide to expand or sell in the future.
- Your financial decisions and forecasts will become increasingly consistent and accurate, as more information will be available to you.

Projections often frustrate new business owners. However, even if your projections aren't initially accurate, you'll be gathering and comparing valuable data—and you'll get better at it! The only way to start is to jump right in.

Total Sales

Projecting total sales is the most crucial and difficult aspect of budgeting. The fact that it is impossible to know how business will be from day to day makes budgeting total sales a perplexing task. Most costs are either variable or semi-variable, which means they will fluctuate directly in relation to the total monthly sales. Thus, accurately projecting these costs depends largely upon using an accurate total sales figure. Projecting total sales, at first, will be difficult—and most likely inaccurate—but after several months of operation, your projections will be right on target. You will be surprised at how consistent sales and customer counts are and how easy it will be to consistently budget accurately.

The initial budgets may be unrealistic expectations. Sales will probably be low, as you will not have been able to build a substantial clientele or reputation. Operating costs will be higher than normal. It will take a couple of months to streamline and build an efficient retail store, even with the best-laid plans. All of these costs are normal and should be anticipated. Profit margins will be small and possibly even nonexistent.

During your startup (or when introducing a new product or launching a new service) allow 4–12 weeks to ensure that your products are perfected and all the bugs are worked out of the system. This is no time to cut back on costs. Your intention is to be in business for a long time. Allocate sufficient funds now to make sure the business gets off on the right foot and profits will be guaranteed for many years.

Schedule a full staff every day to make certain all details will be covered. Discontinue those items that are passable but not of the quality level desired. Slow, clumsy service and only average food will never build sales. Strive for A-1 quality products and service. Constantly reiterate to employees this primary concern, and before long they will self-monitor the quality. Once you develop a clientele and a solid reputation for serving consistent, quality products, the budget and profits will fall into place.

Tracking Sales Growth

If you have purchased an existing retail store, determine the historical sales average by month. This will be your benchmark data. You'll also be able to see a cycle to the sales volume. This information will help you with staff scheduling and purchasing.

When computing and analyzing your retail store activities, keep in mind that each period of time must have the same number and type of days. You can only accurately compare months that have the same number of Mondays, Tuesdays and so forth, since sales are different for each day. That's why some companies use a 13-month calendar for statistical comparisons.

The most accurate way to analyze the percentage of growth or loss is to compare the previous month to the same month last year and then compare the percentage to the current month. Remember to factor in price increases or other variances.

Review and analyze the growth in sales volume during the past year, current year and current month. Based upon past sales figures, determine the percentage of growth or decline in growth anticipated in the coming month. Percentage of growth or decline can be computed by subtracting the most recent period by the past period.

Sales Categories

To compute individual category percentages, divide the category sales by the total daily sales. "Actual Month-to-Date Sales" is a tally of the daily sales. "Cash, Over/Short" refers to any mistakes made at the register. Complimentary, house and manager figures must also be recorded as no-charge sales.

Every item and sale is accounted for and reconciled against every other transaction in the store. Keep all of these forms for at least five years in a fireproof storage file. All forms used during the month may be kept in loose-leaf binders in the bookkeeper's office. If you are using a computerized system, make daily backups and keep copies of monthly backups off-site.

Labor

Manager Salary

Manager salaries should be a fixed monthly cost. Total all the manager salaries for one year; divide this figure by the number of days in the year (usually 365), and multiply this cost by the number of days in one month. Salary changes during the year will require adjustments. When owners take an active part in the management of the store, or when the company is incorporated, the owners should have their salary amount included in this category.

Employee Salary

The employee salary expense is a semi-variable cost that will fluctuate directly with total sales. Employee labor costs have a break-even point, the point where the labor cost is covered by the profit from sales. As this point is reached and total sales increase, the labor cost percentage will decrease, increasing net profit. Thus, the cost of labor is determined by its efficiency and by the volume of sales it produces. Multiply the projected total sales by the average labor cost percentage to arrive at the anticipated labor cost dollar amount. Adjust this figure in relation to the amount of employee training anticipated for the month.

Overtime

Overtime should be nonexistent—or at least kept to an absolute minimum. No amount should be budgeted for overtime. Money spent on overtime usually indicates poor management and inefficiency. Bookkeepers should be on the lookout for employees approaching 40 hours of work near the end of the week. Carefully prepared schedules will eliminate 98 percent of all overtime work and pay. Employees who wish to switch their schedules around should only be allowed to do so after approval from the manager.

Payroll

Getting your employees paid and withholding deposits made accurately and on time can be handled by an in-house bookkeeper with a computerized payroll program or accounting module (such as QuickBooks® or Peachtree®). However, you may find it more convenient to use your accountant, a local payroll service, bank-provided services or a Web-based service.

Although you may decide to use an outside consultant, your bookkeeper will still be involved in the computation of the daily labor costs. After each pay period, the bookkeeper will need to compute each employee's time card and call the information to the payroll service company or key the information into the accounting software. There are time clocks now available that can link employee scheduling, time clock administration and accounting, all into one foolproof system.

Your employees all work for your store; however, you may find it advantageous to calculate their hours and associate them with specific retail activities and/or profit centers. For example: 6 hours stocking shelves and 2 hours handling front counter relief.

The manager and owner salaries should be listed separately at the bottom of the Payroll Form. These costs are separated, as they are budgeted differently.

- The month-to-date payroll percentage is computed by dividing month-to-date sales by the month-to-date actual payroll costs. The budget figures are the budgeted total labor costs divided by the number of days in the month. The month-to-date payroll column is the prorated budgeted amount.

Controllable Operational Costs

Capital Expenditures

Capital expenditures for equipment, vehicles, computers and software can be depreciated over a set lifespan or, under current IRS regulations, may be deducted entirely the year it is purchased. After you launch your business, these costs can be spread out through financing or leasing agreements.

Register Supplies

These are consumable items that need to be replaced frequently. Proper inventory procedures will help you keep these costs down.

Office Supplies

Cost of office supplies should be a fixed dollar amount each month.

Services

Security. Security should be a consistent, fixed monthly expenditure. Service-call charges should be coded to “Equipment Repairs” under “General Operating Costs.”

Freight. Incoming freight charges are usually included in the purchase price. However, you may book charges from an independent carrier for delivery costs.

Legal. Legal service is a variable expense that can fluctuate greatly. Estimates for most legal work can be obtained, but it's best to budget a little each month to cover periodically large legal fees.

Accounting. A semi-fixed expense depending upon the amount and the type of accounting services used. Once set up and operating, the accounting expense should be a consistent monthly charge except for an annual tax-preparation and year-end audit fee.

Maintenance. Facility maintenance should be a fixed monthly expenditure if using a maintenance service company with contract service. This may also include parking lot cleaning, window cleaning and other periodic cleaning services.

Payroll. A semi-fixed expense fluctuating directly with the number of employees on the payroll. Stores not utilizing a computerized payroll service will not have a payroll preparation expense. The wages paid to the bookkeeper are included in the employee labor expenditure.

Utilities

Telephone. Telephone service should be a relatively consistent monthly expense. All long-distance phone calls should be recorded in a notebook (your local office supply store has a specially designed book for this purpose). The itemized phone bill should be compared against the recorded phone calls to justify each one.

Water. Water should be a semi-variable expense.

Gas. Gas may be a variable or semi-variable expense depending upon the type of equipment it operates. Gas used in heating will be a variable expense, because more will be used during the winter months than in the summer.

Electricity. Electricity may be a variable or semi-variable expense depending upon the type of equipment it operates. Electricity bills are normally higher during the summer months, as this is when the air-conditioning units are used.

Heat. Heat includes the cost of any heating material used but not listed above, such as coal, wood, oil, etc.

Fixed Operating Costs

Rent. This should be monthly amount of rent or, if the building is leased, the monthly lease. Certain business-rental and lease agreements also include payment of a percentage of the total sales or per-tax profit amount. Should this be the situation, use the budgeted total sales figure and project the anticipated amount due. Enter this amount and the total rent amount in the "Budgeted" column.

Insurance. Total all insurance premium amounts (fire, theft, liability, workers' compensation, etc.) and divide by 12. This figure will equal the average monthly insurance expense.

Property taxes. If applicable, divide the annual property tax amount by 12. This figure will equal the average monthly property tax amount.

General Operating Costs

Labor taxes. This is the tax amount the employer is required to contribute to the state and federal government. A separate tax account should be set up with your bank to keep all the tax money separate. Labor taxes include: Social Security, federal unemployment tax and state unemployment tax.

Other taxes. This includes all miscellaneous taxes, such as local taxes, sales tax paid on purchases, etc. This column is for any tax the store pays for goods and services. It is not for sales tax or other taxes the store collects, as they are not expenditures. Federal income tax is not a deductible expenditure and should not be listed here either.

Repairs: Equipment. This includes the cost of scheduled and emergency repairs and maintenance to all equipment. Always budget a base amount for normal service. Adjust this figure if major repairs or overhauls are anticipated.

Repairs: Building. This includes the cost of minor scheduled and emergency repairs and maintenance to the building. Always budget a base amount for normal repairs and maintenance. Large remodeling or rebuilding projects should be budgeted as a separate expenditure and depreciated.

Entertainment. Entertainment expenses are deductible only if the amounts spent are directly related to the active conduct of the business.

Advertising. Advertising includes all the costs of advertising the store (including guest speaker fees, sample programs, your Web site, television ads, radio spots, mailing circulars, newspapers, etc.).

Promotional expense. This is the expense of promotional items with your logo or a sponsorship of sporting events, etc. (many times this will be included in advertising expenses).

Equipment rental. This cost is the expense of either short- or long-term renting of pieces of equipment or machinery.

Postage. This is postage paid for business purposes.

Contributions. These are all contributions paid to recognized charitable organizations.

Trade dues, business associations. This includes dues paid to professional organizations such as local and national retailer associations and business organizations such as the Better Business Bureau. Trade magazine subscriptions should also be entered in this category. Annual fees should be divided by 12 to apportion the cost from the month in which it occurs.

Licenses. This is the expense of all business and government licenses: operating licenses, a health permit, liquor licenses, etc. This expense should also be divided by 12 to apportion the cost from the month in which it occurs.

Credit card expense. Credit card expense can be computed by multiplying the service-charge cost-of-sales percentage by the total projected credit card sales volume.

Travel. Travel includes the expense of ordinary and necessary travel for business purposes for yourself and your employees. Expenses incurred with any customer delivery service would be booked under vehicle expense.

Bad debt. This expense should be nonexistent if the proper procedures for handling credit cards and checks are enforced. Normally, the full amount of a bad debt is a tax-deductible expense. However, you must prove the debt is worthless and uncollectible.

Total net profit. Subtract "Total Budgeted Expenditures" from "Total Sales." The result is the total net profit (or loss). Divide the total net projected profit by projected "Total Sales" to compute the projected "Pre-Tax Net Profit Percentage." Total projected sales minus total material costs will equal the gross profit amount.

Depreciation. Depreciation may be defined as the expense derived from the expiration of a capital assets quantity of usefulness over the life of the property. Capital assets are those assets that have utility or usefulness of more than one year. Since a capital asset will provide utility over several years, the deductible cost of the asset must be spread out over its useful life—over a specified recovery period. The IRS publishes guidelines for the number of years to be used for computing an asset's useful life. Each year a portion of the asset's cost may be deducted as an expense. Your accountant can advise you on the rules and benefits of immediate deductibility of equipment and vehicles as compared to depreciating these.

Some examples of depreciable items commonly found in a store include: office equipment, kitchen and dining room equipment, the building (if owned), machinery, display cases and any intangible property that has a useful life of more than one year. Thus, items such as light bulbs, china, stationery and merchandise inventories may not be depreciated. The cost of franchise rights is usually a depreciable expense.

Business owners reaping acceptable profits should not be lax on monitoring costs. High profits can hide inefficiencies that will surely expose themselves during times of low sales. Many people become cost-control converts only after suffering losses.

20

Basic Cost Control for Retail Operations

Operational Costs and Supplies

When establishing your operational budget, you divided supplies into various categories. Creating an Operational Ordering Form and an Operational Inventory Form will help you keep track of daily activity. Whenever a new product is ordered, enter the new item on both forms. When it comes time to preparing your weekly orders and monthly inventory, you will not miss or forget anything, as all the items will be listed. Certain items may fit into two categories because they are used in several areas of the store. Place the item in the category where it is used the most. This will not affect the cost projection as long as the item is listed in only one category.

Ordering Operational Supplies

Ordering operational supplies must be carefully thought out. Too large of an inventory (back stock) will unnecessarily tie up operating capital. However, you must have enough in reserve to cover the unexpected. Having an employee run out for toilet paper is not cost effective. Your inventory levels are determined by the speed orders can arrive, the quantity discounts and your typical usage from delivery to delivery.

Beginning Inventory

Computing this figure is similar to computing the beginning inventory amount for merchandise. However, there is one difference: The beginning inventory amount for each operational category is the dollar amount that is in storage when the store is totally set up. The reason for this is that operational supplies are projected for each month. When you first open, the cost of setting up the store is considered a one-time start-up cost. Operational costs are, thus, a measure of how well you controlled these costs following start-up. Separating this start-up cost may have some additional tax advantages. Your accountant will be able to advise you on this possibility.

Make More by Spending Less

Profitability in a labor-intensive business is directly related to your ability to control your costs for inventory, overhead and people. Cost control is about collecting, organizing, interpreting and comparing numbers that affect your bottom line and tell you the real story of what is going on in your store. This is not a job that can be easily delegated. Working directly with these figures gives you the ability to react quickly to improve your control methods, purchasing procedures and employee training.

Your first step is to create systems and procedures to gather data. Once you have mastered gathering and analyzing the numbers, you will be able to assess your labor productivity, purchase prices, marketing promotions, new products and competitive strategy.

During your first few months of operation, your data may not be precise; however, you are establishing benchmarks to gauge future activities. If you have purchased an existing store, you should have records from the prior owner that will be your benchmark. Franchise operations will be able to give you data based on historical information from other operations in similar communities.

Profits May Hide Problems

Business owners reaping acceptable profits should not be lax on monitoring costs. High profits can hide inefficiencies that will surely expose themselves during times of low sales. Many people become cost-control converts only after suffering losses; this is shortsighted. The idea of prevention versus correction is fundamental. Prevention occurs through advanced planning. Your primary job is not to put out fires; it has to prevent them—and to maximize profits in the process.

Controlling Costs Works

Controlling costs works because it focuses on getting the most value from the least cost in every aspect of your operation. By keeping costs under control, you can charge less than the competition or make more money from charging the same price.

There are operating advantages and opportunities that are not afforded you if you do not know what you are spending. Moreover, if you don't know what you are spending, you cannot control it. Furthermore, waste often cannot be detected by the naked eye. It takes records and reports—whose meanings you have mastered interpreting—to tell you the size of the inefficiencies that are taking place.

The greater the distance between an owner or manager and the actual daily store operation, the greater the need for effective cost-control monitoring.

This is how chain stores and franchisers keep their eyes on thousands of units around the world.

Cost control is not accounting or bookkeeping: these are the information-gathering tools of cost control. Cost control can be defined by explaining its purposes:

- To provide management with information needed for making day-to-day operational decisions.
- To monitor department and individual efficiency.
- To inform management of expenses being incurred and incomes received and whether they fall within standards and budgets.
- To prevent fraud and theft.
- To provide the ground for the business's goals (not for discovering where it has been).
- To emphasize prevention, not correction.
- To maximize profits, not minimize losses.

Cost control is not a sign of distrust towards the staff. The main purpose of cost control is to provide information about daily operations. Prevention of theft is a secondary function. Cost controls are about knowing how you got to where you are and where you are going.

Interpreting the Numbers

Understanding those numbers means interpreting them. To do this effectively, you need to understand the difference between control and reduction. Control is achieved through the assembly and interpretation of data and ratios on your revenue and expenses. Reduction is the actual action taken to bring costs within your predetermined standards. Effective cost control starts at the top of an organization. Management must establish, support and enforce its standards and procedures.

Here are the primary areas that are central to any retail operation and are, therefore, crucial elements of cost-control records:

Purchasing

Your inventory system is the critical component of purchasing. Before placing an order with a vendor, you need to know what is on hand and how what will be used in a given time.

- Allow for a cushion of inventory so you won't run out between deliveries.
- Compare cost per unit of non-perishables vs. usage to determine whether volume buying makes fiscal sense.
- Once purchasing has been standardized, the manager simply reorders from existing suppliers.
- Records show suppliers, prices, unit of purchase, product specifications, etc. This information needs to be kept on paper.

Receiving

This is how you verify that everything you ordered has arrived.

- Check for correct brands, grades, varieties, quantities, correct prices, etc. Products purchased by weight or count need to be checked.
- Incorrect receivables need to be noted and either returned or credited to your account.

Storage

Proper storage, with regard to temperature, ventilation and freedom from contamination, ensures food products remain in optimum condition until being used.

- Expensive items need to be guarded from theft.
- Well-organized storage will reduce the time it takes to inventory items and minimize "assuming" you have plenty on hand.

Issuing

Procedures for removing inventory from storage are part of the cost-control process.

- Managers have authority to take, or "issue," stock from storage to the appropriate place. This is a much more important aspect of cost control than it seems because without this data, you cannot determine accurate sales figures.

- To calculate your cost of goods sold, you need to know your beginning inventory, how much was sold and your ending inventory.

Measuring

If you sell bulk food products, profits can be lost through improper measuring. For example, bulk whole bean coffees require an accurate scale for control. Invest in equipment that can be recalibrated easily.

Ringing Sales

Every item sold needs to be recorded by computer, cash register or manually.

- It needs to be impossible for anyone use, take or give away any resale item without having the transaction entered into the system. Reinforce that this is not a "distrust" procedure but a profit-analysis procedure. Do not forget to allow for discretionary "giveaways" for customer service purposes.

Cash Receipts

Monitoring sales is crucial to cost controls. Under/over-charging and lost paperwork for custom and will-call orders must be investigated daily. Sales information must be compiled to build a historical financial record. This record helps you forecast the future.

Bank Deposits/Accounts Payable

Proper auditing of bank deposits and charge slips must be conducted.

Effective Cost Control

Cost control is an ongoing process that involves every employee. Establishing easy-to-use systems and procedures and explaining the "why" behind the "because" will make your data collection more accurate. A continuous appraisal of this process is integral to the functioning of your store. There are five key elements to an effective cost-control strategy:

- Planning in advance.
- Procedures and devices that aid the control process.
- Implementation of your monitoring and improvement programs.
- Employee compliance.
- Management's ongoing enforcement and reassessment.

Furthermore, your program should be assessed with the following questions:

- Do your cost controls provide relevant information?
- Is the information timely?
- Is it easily assembled, organized and interpreted?
- Are the benefits and savings greater than the cost of the controls?

Penny Wise, Pound Foolish

This point is especially important. When the expense of the controls exceeds the savings, that is waste, not control. Spending $30,000 on a computer system that will save you $5,000 in undercharges is a poor use of your resources.

Setting Standards

Standards are key to any cost-control program. Predetermined points of comparison must be set, against which you will measure your actual results. The difference between planned resources and resources actually used is the variance. Management can then monitor for negative or positive variances between standards and actual performance and will know where specifically to make corrections. These five steps illustrate the uses of standards:

- Performance standards should be established for all individuals and departments.
- Individuals must see it as the responsibility of each to prevent waste and inefficiency.
- Adherence—or lack of adherence—to standards must be monitored.
- Actual performance must be compared against established standards.
- When deviations from standards are discovered, appropriate action must be taken.

Your job is to make sure standards are adhered to. Are shelves always stocked, perishable inventory rotated properly or lights left on unnecessarily in the storage rooms?

Cost Ratios

Owners and managers need to be on the same page in terms of the meaning and calculation of the many ratios used to analyze food, beverage, and labor costs. It is important to understand how your ratios are being calculated so you can get a true indication of the cost or profit activity in your store. Numerous cost-control software programs are available with built-in formulas for calculating ratios and percentages.

Ready-to-Eat Food Sales

If you sell food or beverages meant for immediate consumption, you will need to review your food-cost ratio. This basic ratio is often misinterpreted because it can be calculated so many ways. Basically, it is food cost divided by food sales. In addition, for your food-cost percentage to be accurate, a month-end inventory must be taken. Without this figure, your food-cost statement is basically useless. This is because your inventory will vary month to month—even in the most stable environment (which yours probably won't be initially)—because months end on different days of the week.

Distinguishing between food sold and consumed is important because all food consumed is not sold. Food consumed includes all food used, sold, wasted, stolen or given away to customers and employees. Food sold is food bought at full price.

Sales Analysis

Sales mix is the number of each menu item sold. This is crucial to cost analysis because each item impacts food cost differently. If your competition does a huge breakfast business, and the one down the street does a big lunch, your food costs are going to be different than theirs.

Break-even point is simply when sales equal expenses, period. Businesses can operate forever at break-even; however, you won't be building a business with long-term value.

Profit Analysis

Contribution margin is sales revenue less variable costs. Closing point is when the cost of being open for a given time period is more expensive than revenue earned. This means that if it cost you $2,000 to open today, and you only made $1,800, your closing point expense will be $200.

Pricing

Prices that are too high will drive customers away, and prices that are too low will kill your profits. However, pricing is not the simple matter of an appropriate markup over cost; it combines other factors as well.

Price can be either market-driven or demand-driven. Market-driven prices must be responsive to your competitors' prices. Common items that both you and your competitors sell need to be priced competitively. This is also true when you're introducing new items where a demand has not been developed. Opposite to these are demand-driven items, which customers ask for and where demand exceeds your supply. You have a short-term monopoly on these items; therefore, the price is driven up until demand slows or competitors begin to sell similar items.

However you determine your prices, the actual marking up of items is an interesting process. A combination of methods is usually a good idea, since each product category is usually different. Two basic theories are: 1) charge as much as you can, and 2) charge as little as you can. Each has its pluses and minuses. Obviously, if you charge as much as you can, you increase the chance of greater profits. You do, however, run the risk of losing customers because they won't think you are offering a good value. Charging the lowest price you can gives customers a great sense of value, but lowers your profit margin per item. In a "gourmet" image retail store, low prices can also reduce the perception of quality.

Prices are generally determined by competition and demand. Your prices must be in line with the category customers put you in. You want your customers to know your image and your prices to fit into that picture.

Here are four ways to determine prices:

- **Competitive pricing.** Simply based on meeting or beating your competitions' prices. This is an ineffective method, since it assumes shoppers/diners are making their choice on price alone, and not food quality, ambiance, service, etc.

- **Intuitive pricing.** This means you don't want to take the time to find out what your competition is charging, so you are charging based on what you feel customers are willing to pay. If your sense of the value of your product is good, then it works. Otherwise, it can be problematic.

- **Trial-and-error pricing.** This is based on customer reactions to prices. It is not practical in terms of determining your overall prices, but can be effective with individual items to bring them closer to the price a customer is willing to pay, or to distinguish them from similar menu items with a higher or lower food cost.

- **Psychological pricing.** Price is more of a factor to lower-income customers who go to lower-priced stores. If they don't know an item is good, they assume it is if it's expensive. If you change your prices, the order in which buyers see them also affects their perceptions. If an item was initially more expensive, it will be viewed as a bargain, and vice versa.

Psychology of Pricing

Understanding the psychology of your customers will help you balance these "emotional" judgments. Below are some resources to learn more about pricing psychology to increase sales and profits.

- Purchase the *Pricing Psychology Report* available at www.pricingpsychology.com.
- Check out The Retail Navigator at www.retailnavigator.net.
- Read advice at *PsychoTactics* at www.psychotactics.com/index.htm.

Other Pricing Factors

There are still other factors that help determine prices. Whether customers view you as a leader or a follower can make a big difference on how they view your prices. If people think of you as the best gourmet retail shop in the area, they'll be willing to pay a little more for your wares. Service also determines people's sense of value. This is even truer when the difference in actual product quality and selection between you and the competition is negligible. In a competitive market, providing great service can be the very factor that puts you in a leadership position and allows you to charge a higher price. Your location, ambience, customer base and product presentation all factor into what you feel you can charge and what you need to make a profit.

Financial Analysis

In order to make profits, you need to plan for profits. Many retail stores offering great products in a great location with great service still go out of business. The reason for this is they fail to manage the financial aspects of the business. This means that poor cost-control management could be fatal to your business. Furthermore, good financial management is about interpreting financial statements and reports, not simply preparing them.

A few distinctions need to be made in order to understand the language we are now using. Financial accounting is primarily for external groups to assess taxes, the status of your establishment, etc. Managerial accounting provides information to internal users that becomes the basis for managing day-to-day operations. This data is very specific, emphasizes departmental operations and uses non-financial data such as customer counts, product mix and labor hours. These internal reports break down revenues and expenses by department and time periods so they can be easily interpreted and areas that need attention can be seen. Daily and weekly reports must be made and analyzed in order to determine emerging trends.

Shrinkage

What is politely referred to in the retail industry as "shrinkage" is actually theft, fraud and errors. Employee theft accounts for 46 percent of these losses.[4] Other shrinkage categories are shoplifting at 31 percent, administrative error at 17 percent and vendor fraud at 6 percent.

Clearly established and followed controls can reduce this percentage. Begin by separating duties and recording every transaction. If these basic systems are in place, then workers know that they will be held responsible for shrinkage.

In tightly run establishments, cash is more likely to be taken by management than hourly workers, because managers have access to it and know the system well. Hourly workers tend to steal stuff, not cash, because that's what they can get their hands on. Keeping products away from the back door and notifying

[4] University of Florida study.

your employees when you are aware of theft and are investigating can have a deterring effect.

The key to statistical control, however, is entering transactions into the system. This can be done electronically or by hand. Five other cost-control concepts are crucial to your control system:

1. Require documentation of tasks, activities and transactions.
2. Supervise and review employees by management intimately familiar with set performance standards.
3. Split duties so no single person is involved in all parts of the task cycle.
4. Set time standards where all tasks must be done within set time guidelines. Comparisons then are made at established control points and reports made at scheduled times to detect problems.
5. Review cost-benefit relationships. The cost of the benefits must exceed the cost of implementing the controls.

The basic control procedure is an independent verification at a control point during and after the completion of a task. This is often done through written or electronic reports. This verification determines if the person performing the task has authority to do so and meets set standards.

Point-of-sale systems are also helpful for reducing loss. Once initial training and intimidation are overcome, they can seriously reduce the amount of theft and shrinkage in your store.

Purchasing and Ordering

What exactly is the difference? Purchasing is setting the policy on which suppliers, brands, grades and varieties of products will be ordered. These are your standardized purchase specifications; the specifics of how items are delivered, paid for, returned, etc., are negotiated between management and distributors. Basically, purchasing is what you order and from whom. Ordering, then, is simply the act of contacting the suppliers and notifying them of the quantity you require. This is a simpler, lower-level task.

Once your product choices meet your customers' satisfaction and your profit needs, a purchasing program designed to assure your profit margins can be developed. An efficient purchasing program incorporates standard purchase specifications based on quality, availability and turnaround times.

Once these criteria are met, to order the necessary supplies, your operator needs to be able to predict how much will be needed to maintain purchase specifications, follow standard recipes and enforce portioning standards. When these are done well, optimum quantities can be kept on hand.

Buying also has its own distinctions. Open or informal buying is face-to-face or over-the-phone contact and uses largely oral negotiations and purchase specifics. In formal buying, terms are put in writing, and payment invoices are stated as conditions for price quotes and customer service commitments. Its customer service is possibly the most important aspect of the supplier you choose, because good sales representatives know their products, have an understanding of your needs and offer helpful suggestions.

21

Controlling Your Labor Costs

Labor costs and turnover are serious concerns in today's retail market. Increasing labor costs cannot be offset by continuously higher prices without turning customers away. Maximizing worker productivity so few can do more has become a key challenge for store managers. This is especially important in an industry dominated by entry-level jobs for the unskilled and uneducated. If qualified applicants are hard to find, you'll need to "create" your own.

Manage Time Wisely

The key to controlling labor costs is not a low average hourly wage, but proper scheduling of productive employees. Schedule your best employees during peak periods when you'll need them the most. This requires knowing the strengths and weaknesses of your employees. Staggering the arrival and departure of employees is a good way to follow the volume of expected customers and minimize labor costs during slow times.

- **On-call scheduling.** When your forecasted customer volume data is inaccurate, scheduled labor must be adjusted up or down to meet productivity standards. Employees simply wait at home to be called if they are needed for work. If they don't receive a call by a certain time, they know they're not needed. Employees prefer this greatly to coming in only to be sent home when business is slow.

Creating Productivity

A few of the causes of high labor costs and low productivity are poor layout and design of your store, lack of labor-saving equipment, poor scheduling and an inadequate (or ignored) system to collect and analyze payroll data. The following are some suggested ways management could improve these areas for greater efficiency.

So often in the retail industry, the solution to high labor costs is to lay off employees, lower wages or cut back on hours and/or benefits. These shortsighted measures will initially trim your labor cost, but over time, they will also result in lower overall productivity, a decrease in quality and service, low morale and a high turnover rate. Occasionally some employees may have to be laid off due to a drastic decrease in sales or to initial over hiring, but this should only rarely occur.

Controlling the store's labor cost takes daily management involvement. It cannot be accomplished with one swift action at the end of each month. Described below are some practical suggestions that may be used to streamline your operation so that it may run more efficiently, effectively and profitably.

Design and Equipment

An efficiently designed store with laborsaving equipment is by far the most effective way to reduce labor costs. After several months of operation, examine the store in action. Look at each employee: What are his or her motions and movements? How many steps must be taken to reach food items and more stock? Look at the position and layout of the equipment: Is it set up the most efficient way possible? Ask the employees how they would like their work areas set up, and how work areas could be made more efficient.

They are the real experts—they work the same job every day. Look at your staff's work areas: Could they be made more efficient? These investigations and their results will create faster and better service.

The initial capital expenditures for new equipment can be financed over several years. The cost (less salvage value) can be deducted over several years as a tax-deductible depreciation expense. There are also capital investment incentive deductions where you can write-off the entire purchase during the first year. Be certain to ask your accountant about these benefits and whether leasing is a better option for you.

Efficient Work Areas

Here are some suggestions on how you might make your store layout work for your staff. You'll need to concentrate on front-of-the-store and behind-the-scene areas. Efficient work areas reduce movements (reaching and walking), speed the activity and help your staff concentrate on the customer first!

- Break activities into self-contained workstations where tools, equipment, supplies and storage are within easy reach.
- Keep cleaning supplies in a carryall near where they will be used.
- Include plenty of waste receptacles. Divide waste by type if you will be implementing recycling programs. Check with your waste management company on local requirements for segregating glass, metal, paper, etc.
- Create work triangles. Triangle or diamond layouts give quick access to supplies and equipment while reducing steps.
- Draw out traffic maps to minimize unnecessary steps and crisscrossing paths.
- Allow for ample open space. People need to pass, carts rolled, shelving moved, large buckets wheeled and trays lifted.

- Listen to your staff. Service personnel, stock clerks and managers with retail experience can help you create layouts which won't tire them, help them respond quicker and improve morale.

Labor-Saving Equipment

Every year new pieces of equipment, large and small, expensive and inexpensive, are introduced that will save time, labor and energy. Gone forever are the days when cheap labor will replace the need for new modern equipment. Aside from saving additional labor costs, new mechanization will reduce product handling, eliminate work drudgery and make each task—as well as the overall job—more enjoyable for the employee.

Look at different tasks within your store and explore whether there is an affordable machine that would pay for itself in time savings. Don't forget to ask your employees for ideas. They know their jobs and what tasks could be finished faster, better or with less hassle. They may also have experience with equipment used by other retailers that you had never considered. Invest in equipment that is easy to operate, clean and maintain.

Most importantly, include your staff in the decision and implementation process so they understand the benefits of learning how to operate a new tool. If people hate to use it, you may not be saving anything!

22

Leaving Your Retail Business

Rarely do new business owners consider the importance of being able to sell their business. Because no one has a crystal ball, you cannot predict what life event will cause you to sell your store. Building a saleable business is a way to strengthen your return on your initial and future investments. A profitable store can bring top dollar and your profit from the sale is your reward for all the long, hard hours you spent developing it.

The best time to prepare for the future is now! Creating a business that has lasting value means that your hard work will continue to provide you with an excellent income. Your ROI is a healthy retirement nest egg or the capital for a new business venture. Whether you wish to retire, want to move to a new city or have a life challenge that necessitates you sell your store, you will have better control over the situation if you have a prepared exit plan.

Your Exit Plan

Just as you prepared a written business plan, you should create a short exit plan. Do not forget to review and update your plan annually to reflect your current business state and your objectives. Your plan should cover:

- **Your exit desires—best-case scenario.** When do you want to retire? Do you want the business to be sold outright?
- **Your business assessment—current value.** How much could you get in cash if you liquidated or sold it?
- **Ways to enhance your business value.** Have you developed a succession team? Can you increase output or make changes that would make it more attractive to buyers?
- **Worst-case scenario.** What will happen in an emergency?
- **Sales preparedness.** Do you know the tax implications of selling? Could you carry the paper?
- **Bowing out.** Do you know what to do to leave your business to others? to dissolve partnerships or corporations?
- **Family preparedness—securing your family's financial health.** Do you have a will? How will they handle your affairs should you die? Will they be able to run the business without you?

Your attorney and accountant can provide valuable advice in creating your plan. For more information on exit plans, visit:

- Principal Financial Group at www.principal.com/bizprotection/exitplan.htm.
- Family Business Experts at www.family-business-experts.com/exit-planning.html.
- American Express Small Business at www.americanexpress.com/smallbusiness.

Passing On Your Business

Millions of small businesses are family owned and operated. These businesses are passed down through the generations so their legacies continue. Other businesses continue under the guidance of partners or employees.

Issues such as inheritance tax, business trusts and tax-free gifts are all complex issues best left to professionals. Discussing your concerns with your estate planner, banker, accountant and lawyer are critical to ensure a smooth transition and minimize the tax burdens on your family. The U.S. Chamber of Commerce offers advice on passing your business on at www.uschamber.com. CCH Business Owner's Toolkit has several helpful articles at www.toolkit.cch.com.

Grooming Your Replacement

Your business exit scenario may mean that someone else steps into your shows. Grooming a replacement takes time—especially if you and your family will continue to have financial ties to your store. A natural part of your hiring process should be to envision whether this person might be a good successor for your legacy.

If you have a candidate in mind, start by sharing your vision for the future and develop a plan.

- Train on unfamiliar areas.
- Increase their responsibilities.
- Review their decision-making abilities.
- Listen to their needs and ideas.
- Share money management goals.
- Set a timeline for transfer.
- Develop transition stages.
- Set benchmarks and goals.
- Examine and improve "problem" issues.
- Prepare to leave—emotionally and physically.

Selling Your Business to Your Employees

You can sell your business to an employee or group of employees as you would with any potential buyer. This is not without risks, as unless they have ample capital, you most likely will be "underwriting" some of the financing.

There are some caveats as feelings may be hurt when your employees/buyers want to make seemingly random changes to "your way of doing things," and your friendships may become strained when haggling over money. Your attorney and accountant can act as a go-between to keep the selling process professional and less emotionally charged.

Business Law, www.businesslaw.gov, discusses Employee Owned Stock Plans (EOSP) as an option for transferring your business to your employees. National Center for Employee Ownership offers advice at www.nceo.org, and the Beyster Institute for Entrepreneurial Employee Ownership at www.fed.org.

Transferring your business to a worker co-op can have some advantages for everyone. Worker co-op structures are discussed at the National Cooperative Business Association at www.ncba.org. Transferring your ownership to employees (similar to family inheritance) can also be done.

Saying Good-Bye

As an owner/operator of a store, saying good-bye to your employees, your early morning schedule and the realization of your dreams can be hard. Letting go is much easier of you have prepared for the day. You have sacrificed and struggled to build a legacy—it is also your responsibility to preserve it!

23

Resources

Trade Shows and Associations

- All Candy Expo, National Confectioners Association—www.nca-cma.org
- AmericasMart Atlanta—www.americasmart.com
- Barbeque Industry Association—http://hpba.org
- Dallas National Gift & Home Shows, George Little Management—www.glmshows.com/dallas
- Fancy Food & Culinary Magazine—www.talcott.com
- Food Marketing Institute—www.fmi.org
- Gourmet News—www.gourmetnews.com
- Institute of Store Planners—www.ispo.org
- In-Store Marketing Institute—www.instoremarketer.org

- International Daily Deli Bakery Association—www.iddba.org
- International Housewares Association—www.housewares.org
- National Association of Specialty Food Trade—www.specialtyfood-market.com
- National Association of Store Fixture Manufacturers—www.nasfm.org
- National Food Distributors Association—www.specialtyfoods.org
- National Restaurant Association—www.restaurant.org
- National Retail Federation—www.nrf.com
- National Specialty Gift Association—www.nsgaonline.com
- Natural Products Expo—www.naturalproductexpo.com
- New York International Gift Fair, George Little Management—www.nyigf.com
- Retailer News—www.retailernews.com
- Specialty Coffee Association—www.scaa.org
- Tea Association of America—www.teausa.com
- The Gourmet Retailer—www.gourmetretailer.com
- The Wine Institute—www.wineinstitute.org
- Trade Directory of Wholesalers—www.thomasintl.com
- Visual Merchandising Trade Association—www.vmta.org

Index

A

B

C

D

E

F

G

H

I

J

L

M

N

T

U

V

W

We recently lost our beloved pet "Bear," who was not only our best and dearest friend, but also the "Vice President of Sunshine" here at Atlantic Publishing. He did not receive a salary, but worked tirelessly 24 hours a day to please his parents. Bear was a rescue dog that turned around and showered myself, my wife Sherri, his grandparents Jean, Bob and Nancy and every person and animal he met (maybe not rabbits) with friendship and love. He made a lot of people smile every day.

We wanted you to know that a portion of the profits of this book will be donated to The Humane Society of the United States.

–Douglas & Sherri Brown

THE HUMANE SOCIETY OF THE UNITED STATES©

The human-animal bond is as old as human history. We cherish our animal companions for their unconditional affection and acceptance. We feel a thrill when we glimpse wild creatures in their natural habitat or in our own backyard.

Unfortunately, the human-animal bond has at times been weakened. Humans have exploited some animal species to the point of extinction.

The Humane Society of the United States makes a difference in the lives of animals here at home and worldwide. The HSUS is dedicated to creating a world where our relationship with animals is guided by compassion. We seek a truly humane society in which animals are respected for their intrinsic value, and where the human-animal bond is strong.

Want to help animals? We have plenty of suggestions. Adopt a pet from a local shelter, join The Humane Society and be a part of our work to help companion animals and wildlife. You will be funding our educational, legislative, investigative and outreach projects in the United States and across the globe.

Or perhaps you'd like to make a memorial donation in honor of a pet, friend or relative? You can through our Kindred Spirits program. And if you'd like to contribute in a more structured way, our Planned Giving Office has suggestions about estate planning, annuities, and even gifts of stock that avoid capital gains taxes.

Maybe you have land that you would like to preserve as a lasting habitat for wildlife. Our Wildlife Land Trust can help you. Perhaps the land you want to share is a backyard—that's enough. Our Urban Wildlife Sanctuary Program will show you how to create a habitat for your wild neighbors.

So you see, it's easy to help animals. And The HSUS is here to help.

The Humane Society of the United States
2100 L Street NW
Washington, DC 20037
202-452-1100
www.hsus.org